HUGE HAIKU

HUGE HAIKU

DAVID McALEAVEY

chax press

My thanks to the editors of the following publications, where individual poems as indicated either have appeared or will soon appear: "All right okay yes": *Wooden Teeth;* "Back to Piney Hills": *6ix;* "Chimps with lumps of coal": *Transmog;* "Couldn't find the spot": *Situation;* "Feeling pitiful": *Nedge;* "Here's how: gather your": *Situation;* "If there were others": *Washington Review;* "Kissing Emily": *Transmog;* "Mayo ham & cheese": *Ploughshares;* "Mr. Jefferson": *Washington Review;* "Oranges ripen": *Situation;* "Screwed up the contract": *6ix;* "That which is unsaid": *Nedge;* "*The contest between*": *Poetry;* "The sounds of passage": *Indefinite Space;* "What else but fireworks": *Pacific Coast Journal.*

Beltway, an online journal, republished "All right okay yes," "Couldn't find the spot," "Here's how: gather your," "Kissing Emily," "Mayo ham & cheese," and "Mr. Jefferson" on April 3, 2001. Part of "A long dark cavern" was published as "The Greeks had a word" on buses in Northern Virginia (May and June, 2001), as part of the "Moving Words" project of the Arlington County Cultural Affairs program, and was reprinted in the Arlington County Cultural Affairs' division's online newsletter (June 2001).

Thanks as well to the Virginia Center for the Creative Arts (Sweet Briar, Virginia) and Schloß Wiepersdorf (Wiepersdorf, Germany), two artists' colonies where I had very productive residencies leading to the completion of this manuscript.

ISBN 0-925904-46-5

Chax Press
101 W. Sixth St., no. 6
Tucson, AZ 85701-1000
USA

CONTENTS

FOUR

FIVE

SIX

Blunt architecture

blunt architecture   two carbon-arc beams focused   open into night
grounded means punished   well-grounded means disciplined   but a terrier
the tourists return   as detectable from space   as spring, as seasons
it matters to him   he dreams about his golf swing   hitting the sweet spot
cunning often wins   but Odysseus was strong   yes, & loved by gods

cut short by weather   a piano redaction   xeroxed photographs
ordinary air   breathing & knowing vaguely   way inside mountains
inventing mousetraps   not because mice bother you   it's the way we talk
I'm the only one   entitled to use the words   "me," "myself," & "I"
formal wear required   locked inside the city walls   capillary walks
gymnastic squirrels   we watched them mate on our deck   time to plant carrots
grounded means attached   a plaid is just that, plain plaid   resembles the grid

don't ask what it means   it's using big words again   bless you wink wink wink
the life of peasants   medieval in most aspects   animals in sex
peeked around corners   sponging up the atmosphere   never been to Rhodes
such idolatry   his poison Amazon darts   or that or torture
many thousand watts   male rod, gap, female tube, spark   how to make a light

Oranges ripen

oranges ripen   she sets out down the orchard   oranges, and greens
she massages her scalp   generals review their troops   her army's mental
what she overheard,   a recipe for braised heart: since when she's unchanged
seas change (seamlessly   her unaltering strangeness)   a lost tribe's found text
unable to work   she sees sun set into sea   dips her quill pen in

two people hook "up"   any Ann Bob Bill Marie   when then they break "up"
the kids were okay   plastic, meaning they would bounce   not letting force through
in the church of light   hard, they made them kneel for hours   that was long ago
a stiffnecked people   temperance before remorse   vigilant as rocks
rocks as vigilant   Bill loses track of Marie   feel the rough surface
lichen-etched granite   pebbles clattering in streams   rounding each other
silt settling in mouths   what they learn from the torrent   unshaped to new shapes

I tire of satire   you would like to take a trip   we were slap-happy
I finished the tape   you weep and weep, you, you weep   we had two problems
I thought I'd find love   you prefer the newer wine   we like to fly, thanks
I had the salmon   you know how to whip a horse   we grind corn for bread
I touch the moon's face   you surround yourself amply   we whisk by; others

Giants in short sleeves

giants in short sleeves   the north coast of New Zealand   walking into waves
read this before that   aiming for disappointment   crumbs in the keyboard
bones in the closet   so far the ride's too bumpy   spine-cracking delight
making ideas   from bits & dust & dumb luck   making it all up
here's a plan: pressed snake: talking with him, you forget   you're dreaming again

in a news release   accompanying photo   they're on a nude beach
the thing they made's gone   leapt from the bay in a skip   sailing soda cans
linked like DNA   all that cross-bred local noise   July isotherms
vanished, is the word   & the speckled throat stickles   (whoso draws from dream
what a way to be   in her singlet no guitar   slash/catastrophe
who likes or won't like   "let me see if I can come"   to spit-roast a goose
it's long gone by now   too bad you had to miss it   it took off & flew

before before now   hair is a hurricane watch   crimes in the keyboard
typos postulate   I'm sorry it has to be   right in the middle
gamma reduction   in spring the frogs whatever   at last what you meant
please don't just dry up   once one, always a raisin   *thrips* is too loony
you're slimy my dear   just a thing to take up space   why it won't collapse

Sanctum sanctorum

sanctum sanctorum   to define opening out   gallons of honey
I never used to   so readily tearing up   getting fragile or
loose re-entry tiles   or else I've grown enormous   a fairy-ring ring
circular mushroom   only able to expand   away from its past
and if succeeding   kilometers of tissue   probably broken

3 blind mice & no   body denies, no wizard: DREAM ARCHITECTURE:
so listen to this: the house was old, remodeled   not exactly mine
but mine, & upstairs   I was there with a woman   both wife and sister
sleeping fitfully   the smoke detectors go off   the house is on fire
it's a split-level   I've never lived in this house   I find the kitchen
on a pantry shelf   there's a fire extinguisher   just like my real house
& under the sink   I can sense somewhere the flames   as if reflected

as for my parents   they live downstairs, the ground floor   I'm hoping somehow
they are getting out   this little extinguisher   surely won't save them
the house is on fire   okay maybe it's not mine?   *your house is your life*
your sister's your wife   *your parents are your parents*   *the whole thing's burning*
what is there to save?   re-entry, vaporizing   to be continued

Watch Hilary write

watch Hilary write   during her studio time   po•etry display
coffee in a mug   many rings of black inside   Bobby fixes cars
a three-dollar set?   wonders Anita-waitress   or more? (nude dancer!)
incidentally   Jim's cup has a frog in it   computer jock trick
Mark negotiates   so do Rick, Skip, Bill, Marie   we all get along

Chris is a runner   his dad let his own health go   working for his kids
the same thing for Jack   whose dad's heart//the old story   he exercises
& how about Ed   spine nerve junk and glaucoma   swimming at eighty
at the grocery   Bhopi, her forearm splinted   carpal tunnel woes
o womb, o belly   Nono's in the hospital   angioplasty
plus endoscopy   he turns out to have cancer   here's a get-well card
Laurie can't go out   running with her allergies   so she swims I guess

Gayle's here in DC   her guy's up in New Jersey   she sees lots of trains
Ken has a new life   moved to Silicon Valley   got engaged to Fran
up in Seattle   Becky's settled down with Chris   making commitments
Barbara's new friend   she wouldn't tell me his name   maybe he's famous
since Jeff got divorced   he just talks about himself   testing your friendship

Not a resentnik

not a resentnik   he said but my job's less swell   my merits grand, *viz.*:
I'm in better shape   I know more & work harder   & I'm way hipper
my vices worser   technology more advanced   my name known widely
supercharged & bad   & jazz a bonus fillip   my harmonica
— I was a c.o. —   — just because I was drafted —   — others cut in line —

what it is, cocks preen   not a legal holiday   not a job action
to negate his pride   from other repercussions   stacked canteloupes fall
an intimate sphere   when she wore a garterbelt   the skin space between
there's a hot white light   don't talk promises to me   they studied plumbing
don't besmirch scoring   not the double-pump technique   wills meeting through flesh
she guided a hand   the jets revving & squealing   torch lit by a touch
now there's a story   ate brisket and potatoes   walked by the winners

botanic skyways   a fine bevy of autos   Topkapi Palace
advise consumers   large-ticket items shot up   slower on high-tech
curtains dropped on trust   economics winterland   why do I feel *feel*
bread's being eaten   elevators for whole ships   a granary thing
possible highjack   all he wants is a quickie   easy to renege

I want to tell you

I want to tell you   warmer, a light rain, walking   still walking, at dawn
here where you have it   brands mark most gear of the times   even eyeglasses
used to see the world   so baby what does it mean   tree frogs will be next?
burly confidence   containers her expertise   can't total columns
scrupled over it?   they look down elegantly   won't lift a finger

am supremely here   like nobody's business   palm fronds in winter
frightened by dreamwork   *tranquilly Titicaca*   reads the rest right here
remarkable stunts   thing about sex about now   who trimmed his hedges
no such thing as half   redirected that message   presentiment reeks
arrows his own way   embraceable allergy   frightened by the dark
frightened by repeats   she meant well; she meant the best   they work in motels
up in beside you   purloined the surface details   it all means it it

so for a story: I was watching a movie   then I had to leave
up from the basement   up steep out a tiled canal   you doubt you'll make it
you've done it before   this time there's glass at the top   rich folks gaping down
here's a place to stop   explaining why you go on   lost my buffalo
lost my keys, my car   speaking to you from the grave   squeezed, got juice, *did not*

They keep asking him

they keep asking him   how do you like our new space   fine, he says, OK
it's an alleyway   a junction of alleyways   but at night who knows
they sell furniture   huge mahogany tables   leather-covered chairs
is it code they speak?   he's not getting much of it   he edges away
they rise abruptly   cover their stuff with brown tarps   others are coming

he's out with a girl   she's young, she likes to take drugs   he doesn't know that
guns are lips, knives tongues,   she waits for him in the car   he's got business
you want to try this?   a tight thin joint comes his way   roach clip included
later to a club   the act's an old guy who sings   has a *claim* to fame
downtown seems foreign   all the bars have funny names   stones & cobblestones
he gets transported   it didn't happen by plan   out by the freeway
he walks out of there   children and dogs hanging on   to them he's safety

a pharaonic brew   ended in *reductio*   he opens that pub
to practice dancing   to help right now the homeless   to let slip away
to lift weights, to run   to be a sports announcer   to be messiah
spelled it perfectly   the African genesis   escaped by cable
by wicker basket   *tight spot* the theme of the month   there's still snow down there

Subjects lost in words

subjects lost in words   she danced inside a balloon   inside a balloon
telling polka jokes   why no it's an elegy   a worm in the bean
my calliope   (a poet's not a juke box)   a few cruddy pipes
we prefer Pampers   putting something on the line   as did the Buddha
here's an idea   we'll display the crown jewels   as did the Buddha

she danced in balloons   voluptuous to the eye   what would you ask her
you don't augur well   it's not about auguring   it's about having
first pre-Cambrian   (two times the dust of old hills)   then sunrise we say
organized lyrics   a union in unison   so to speak to so
no rage in mirage   [listen, now that we're alone]   may I be honest?
"aum" is my mantra   now we're friends, we say goodbye   Lenny did my chart
I unwrap your gifts   "Ram" showed me his holy rock   you could share the fire

he used a French curve   a way to shape elastic   those people have died
which is poverty   which is the mansion we're in   let's count the fishes
on to the ball then   my friend's a sexy dancer   her guy waves a *kris*
yes, try gardening   I don't think you need to hide   I think you can't hide
unsource me who can   at last, the news of the world   a bird wheeks & wheeks

Here's how: gather your

here's how: gather your   seed-roots-berry assortment   dry it in the sun
a star's aloofness   assembling & combusting   happens to shuck "light"
in inventory   has the year brought anything   but bad news and books?
find a nice flat stone   maybe two feet long, one wide   but flat's important
phone call re: divorce   played a game with *death*'s letters   morose denial

the gate is tilting   clunk: the dog drops his big stick   their window's still dark
find another stone   one you can hold with both hands   having a flat side
the campground's assigned   enter this stream where you please   faking dictators
now's a day of rest   unweaponed himself at last   eating irises
here's how: they quarreled   soon enough the land they owned   returned to nature
it's OK to ask   you wanted South African   you got Chilean
crush a small handful   pound & push & pull again   till you get ground meal

brought his lexicon   organic food supermart   big-prize radishes
too busy to think   able to do wave physics   to love opera
to detect a lie   both parties drowned while struggling   slipping to neutral
the ball fluttered by   a long and desperate kick   the stands now empty
mix in some water   put it on a stone near fire   this tastes great tonight

Ew that's gross *ew ew*

ew that's gross *ew ew*   the land's watery margin   a noisy gnawing
lax to have stretched out   hand over the pictograph   like a robbery
call this a workshop   because of piled *rejecta*   discarded flint chips
to have rock to work   blew up//into a riot   or rite//quarry right
genital landscape   Michelangelo something   don't be so droopy

now you've got the plot   so to speak the hang of it   you'd thought she'd be sweet
let's talk in a field   I've a mind to, but won't, hurt   good Anglo-Saxon
we wanted a nook   a hollow where the stream runs   shade from a broad tree
morning intervenes   would you like a bran muffin   an aisle-voice speaking
your world's so pretty   gleaming chrome, piped hall music   *ew! comma-dating!*
Choose "Associate"   with my ore to fill your rifts   & lists out his strengths
which marks the end of   words you hate to have to hate   choose not to recite

gentle Nan née Bangs   I'm thinking about crying   her name a sentence
o trophy trophy   on the wall who's the fairest...   Say you HATE PLATO
soon to be April   a map of Jerusalem   new maintenance sheds
mixed & matched & matched   like Mr. Potato Head   the woman he loves
the man she adores   her soiled J. Crew catalog   they've gone out hunting

Already with thee

already with thee   what thou lovest well remains   ever fixèd mark
ending of winter   Orion low in the west   snowdrops, crocuses
: not random sleuthing   : try exposing her motive   : she's such a show-off!
she won't always laugh   he wins who makes her guffaw   Courtship 101
pentasyllabic   add two: heptasyllabic   back to base (*penta*)

applied to travel   wrote monologues for Johnny   outlawed the Beatles
from Slovakia   Dire wolf dreams, extinct Dire wolves   uncuddly Cave bears
fed a formula   extorted love and lawn chairs   my orality
my name is Eugene   *I have a Geiger counter*   *an adding machine*
he lived right next door   unpredicted suicide   *an Osterizer*
a color TV   *the first of everything*   *glasses for 3-D*
a tan Chihuahua   in his yard he drilled for oil   had fled the Nazis

music overhead   no we're not living alone   the black cat's greeting
you have had a past   that's the basis for you here   a lovely process
it won't stay focused   I hate what this is about   I'm not being shy
a clay pot will break   exactly what works better   the Finger, writing
it takes a whole day   I need my onion bagel   how we got along

What am I thinking

what am I thinking   the ground's so full of water   digging these small holes
pretty sloppy work   flowerpot-size hand-dug wells   water seeps & fills
I come back at night   under moonlight, a swiss cheese,   polkadots of light
after days of rain   I've made a huge colander   catching at the moon
each hole clocks itself   mud-junk sinks, clear water stays   my hand goes in clear

thought about earth-art: I love dirt; all art's earth-art: *We are all star-stuff*
thought about settling: *Lord, what fools these mortals be*   heavy dross sinks fast
thought about floating: bits of grass-chaff swirl on top   in time, soak and sink
thought about earth art: cairns of recall/graves of grief: to tunnel through walls
thought about floating: *wild deer Startle, and stare out*   eye's image reflects
thought about settling: I see my hand descending   made odd, refracted
thought about earth art: to breathe's leaving — & joining —   to dig down's to raise

you can poke me too   at any point I'll brim up   I'm no tough surface
I had a dream once   I remember the found flesh   orange & squishy
you could push on it   like it was dehydrated   it would hold the mark
(an Orpheus dream   — exploring his living grave —   half a life ago)
I can't say what's wrong   maybe at last nothing's wrong   *Daylight come, and I*

Soft-contour mapping

soft-contour mapping   it's done with mere fingertips   your room can't be cold
e. g., he "maps" her   we love to sort mysteries   she's mysterious
whose complicity   or frenzied hysterical   hunting the ribald
there's a bug in here   snaky-tongued frogs taking aim   which simplicity
fog over the hills   PEOPLE HAVE TO LIVE IN THIS?   (it could seem lucky)

without medicine   they'd have stopped it long ago   all their complaining
conscious animals   who saw halos to invent?   a time before "that,"
back before language   being screwed up is not like   *Alles in Ordnung*
eased her chaos-fear   leased the new Cadillac-guy   washed it, wrapped it tight
I know what you think   elegant, wearing home-mades   knew the reviewers
they hopped over here   important Math Olympics   wooed, rebuffed, ran off
reversed his command   it's a fly at the window   (ate it with pesto)

people love in this?   first, if it's cold, raise the heat   touch-anthrography
here I am again   again making sense again   time to take your pill
we *like* mysteries   what if Earth just broke apart?   *the experts agree*
calm down. meditate.   of known parents *which are you?*   CDs improved sound
this is the last time   leave the flies alone, or else   (I'm such a magnet)

To get from point A

to get from point A   to begin to leave point A   not knowing point B
MY dictionary!   *vanilla, venal, vinyl*   where'd *vehicle* go?
to have to leave A   never having truly known   A's side-streets, bus-stops
here's *ventricular*   now use it in a sentence   "*Ventricular fibs.*"
too soon to grow up   to make my own way away   to find a new A

very good *varies*   hands off, those are MY *varies*   *veal* is upsetting
the problem with A   you're lucky to get away   tiny A's too small
velocity works   instead of diminishing   liftoff into *veils*
I'll never leave A   the point of my life is A   my dreams are of A
before the Romans   such a beautiful *valley*   a pastel *vista*
I can't think of B   all I've ever known is A   its smiles & storefronts
veer and *vole* of course   you "stake" a claim (or *vampire*)   I'm mining MY mine

maybe A's a dream   or stands for Arbitrary   or just Adequate
here it's all *velure*   or *vilify, violins*   more empty *V*-signs
I salute A's flag   I'd never join B's army   that's what loyal is
vixen, which *vixen*   there by the side of the road   a final *version*
if A *vanishes*   as in perspectives, points do   —born again at B?

Our beautiful vet

our beautiful vet   wanted to alter Dylan   hopeless we said yes
he'd never mated   though children a certain size   always were targets
he'll be gentler now   no nostalgias I suppose   dreams growing vaguer
lost his *cojones*   become the butt of bad jokes   otherwise unchanged
emasculated   yes, but no *castrati* voice   he still barks the same

the subject changes   to use the dime-wide ledges   *technical climbing*
not that this is safe   it's expecting resistance   offers thin shelter
how it's gotten here?   that's what it's a record of   you follow its track
maybe you like plains   maybe you like scenic views   or why not orchards
mountainside orchards   abandoned to woodpeckers   gray glacier-melt streams
you don't know the rules?   *praxis* first, not etiquette   & get the right gear
where we've been going   touching the unspoken ground   at every step

aging but still spry   ready to dance through the night   they R.S.V.P.
why it's called a ball?   the couples go round and round   as if thrown or kicked
wave your arms, people!   when you get stuck in traffic   look like Mr. Fun
music radio   helps us out of a tight spot   into avoidance
cosmic thumb-pressure   limbs much too heavy to run   a bad dream for sure

Carpenter's levels

carpenter's levels: liquid sealed in a glass tube   with an air bubble
mounted rigidly   in a straight flatbottomed frame   normally metal
I've got an antique   iron rails with curlicues   it sits there retired
I've got a new one   stiff aluminum I-bar   it helped build a fence
well now those are tools   we've been sloshing around here   called spirit levels

here's an example   words which make sense together   virtue rewarded
the pretty bubble   centered in its windowframe   at least something true!
that is, vertical   or horizontal, that is,   relative to earth
to this spot, this cold   crust of earth with gravity   to contend against
but it's also true   come intuit this with me   the bubble will slip
who knows Newton's rules   temporarily away   is it modesty
a delicate mind   to avoid the straight sunlight   walks into darkness

for many people   the goal's equilibrium   as it is for me
the pretty bubble!   visible where it belongs!   as it seems to me
but the other thing   the thing we can't really see   past the window's edge
sure the bubble's there   spirit foreteller & guide   unoriented
out of the howling   syllables something wildly   buttons, a red dress

TWO

Used secondaries

used secondaries   roadmaps unreliable   hard hills & dead ends
anxious dogs angry   I think about self-defense   I carry nothing
here's my strategy: get off the bike speak calmly   the bike makes a shield
maybe pepper spray   I'll ask the local bike shop   *who goes with Fergus?*
off the long pastures   a cool vegetable breeze   blue mountains profiles

/a doing occurs   /doing is what's happening   /doing more occurs
as in appetite   like ancient philosophy?   no — dream furniture —
why then I'll fight you   right here in the arena   just sky for witness
in a truc haiku   false dead ends leaf; bloom; fruit falls   (green blackwalnut balls)
that book's hereabouts   defines with authority   mashed all the grass flat
suppose you relax   your spiritual hereness   I've cleared you a space
fragrances & oils   attars, perfumes, & esthers   synthesized a self

take this book with you   I'm going beyond that wall   I've got stuff to do
we'll join up again   I name stumbling my virtue   it proves I'm attached
I own three t-shirts   of many, three showing bikes   a mountain bike one
a Baltimore one   & the DC bike tour one   I'll need new ones soon
centripetal force   unifies but what's moving's   subterfuge and gone

A jazz diversion

a jazz diversion   about the only music   well now it's broken
tin slivers of it   arching and silent present   worth vitalizing
so much of music   loose abundant arpeggios   & the geese & crows
shredded harmony   cows & snakes & cottontails   children's animals
earliest observed   you study all your life to see: or never master

how do you hear jazz?   *exactly!* by listening!   (they heard him whistling)
catch the pause coming?   now, farther off, another?   and now, a full stop
or traveling down   varying complexities   in disposing time
the sheer drop of life   always on to the next thing   sometimes gets garbled
meets a useful haze   accepts a little training   goes from side to side
then plateaus or pools   turns out to a waterfall   an end which begins
you ask how to read   *again*'s maybe the answer   or: what ways make sense

DNA something   followed by DUI or   DWI
then there's B & E   for which if you're caught you might   see things with bars on
but there's worse to come   feloniousness, my word!   let's sneak out the back
WHEW! MUCH better now   out here in the back barnyard   stray music units
a breeze, & bee stings   no trace of the comics store   yes a mockingbird

Mayo ham & cheese

mayo ham & cheese   *mayonnaise, jambon, fromage*   lettuce, tomato
two slices wheat bread   golden delicious apple   pack of snack crackers
iced tea in the fridge   (instant) or if you prefer   instant lemonade
they feed us too well   not that I'm getting worried   I'm enjoying camp
I think I'll come back   that's better than misery   better than despair

someone claims Braque said: *I should be utterly lost   if I knew where I*
was going; that *If   you know where you are going   you will surely not*
get there was said by   Leonardo; that Tolstoy   said, *What you may not*
have above all in   making a novel is pre-   conception; and that
Picasso once said,   *I find first, seek afterward.*   someone else says it's
Brancusi who said,   *Things are not difficult to   make; what's difficult*
is putting ourselves   in the state of mind to make   them. — these give us hope —

kind of you to ask   yes, my heart's a checkerboard   with some darker parts
you have spoken well   we must be more wary now   too much is tacit
& then violent   has your lover never beat   or bit or scratched you?
let us pray for peace   that peace may descend from clouds   of full divulgence
& then when we play   no one needs to take the role   of mere dumb body

I think you'll like this

I think you'll like this   stylotherapy mama   winsome lassoer
painted his model   painted her out via green   left a round diamond
why don't you tell me   a little language of tongues   meaning "criminy"?
she was laugh laughing   it's easy for another   bees hit the clover
bees hit the clover   drawing room: hence a novel   winched into the well

my father's father   comfortable with women   cars, booze, cards, cigars
liked being Irish   but not being Catholic   what did he believe?
his ambitious wife   a German farm family   gave it up at last
chased him w/ a knife   Dad said a big butcher's knife   chased around the house
but before all that   according to my mother   there was the sister
they don't use her name   Annie, maybe; anyway   Dad's younger sister
from diabetes   died at five six or seven   though strong and pretty

in my family   men haven't been forgiven   honoring the grudge
I heard a bobwhite   the story of a brave girl   who frees the wizard
clover and thistles   I'm so gentle domestic   you can't have heard me
rusting cattle guards   crumbling asphalt regraveled   I think you'll like this
we exchanged money   it was for the laundromat   the disguise of clean

That which is unsaid

that which is unsaid   obvious without choosing   choosing to unsay
a bird bangs windows   who thought of this as playing   I was taking drops
it's not so hard but   what follows *d* is taboo   but *f* is okay
swing impositions   giving up a laxity   no fondling of Puss
still glass clarity   is that all you can think of   no, his hand-built bass

here, now, I relent   I'll write no book without *e*   now I'll be able
to write the right name   a *bee* whom I struck riding   stung me on my thigh
I could have written   *wasp* and so avoided *e*   and you wouldn't care
but it still itches   what itches most is the scar   from a pus-filled boil
it's been hard to find   I'd even forgotten it   joy's not what I feel
warmed by bee's toxin   the birds are hitting windows   the world comes at us
the world's encroaching   we're responding, transforming   for whom the bee toils

interconnected   but as for you my pathos   reading half-anxious
yes I'm confident   if bees can sting I can swell   I swell up like you
looking side by side   my isn't this a strange land   ghost anxieties
we see what we mean   a chandelier in the sky   a good sweet desert
that's not a typo   yes I'm thinking of crying   not harder than you

Voluptuousness

voluptuousness   a thing you never measure   tiny downy nests
last night in a line   geese honked across the steeple   does Bill play bells there
I'm easily swayed   joined Free Radicals Fan Club   made concrete coffins
who was explaining   explaining is beautiful   I'm striking off now
something hurt me once   something really hurt me once   not a flycatcher

I'm neighbor to tears   I always try to earn love   I KNOW it won't work
they respect me fine   they give me pretty presents   I keep quite busy
I KNOW I must yield   *Wie meinst du das* you could say   to do will away
to will will away   it's like walking past roses   pretty but thorny
all along the road   face the traffic, walk the edge   a prickly byway
not that bad really   at some point you say OK   trust somebody else
but those are my eggs   but let your spouse take a turn   there's an example

it's all eggs today   ugh, I hope you're not POACHING   I gave and you took
only it wasn't   you didn't give me a thing   later you were bored
I like rocks with stripes   I know how they got those lines   rocks are so patient
an interruption   it's no hairy confession   *loved I not honor*
look me in the eye   told my story with stained glass   not faith exactly

Someone's teakettle

someone's teakettle   the dormitory kitchen   who'll turn the heat off
I've chased you gamely   I guess it's pretty funny   definitively
I chase and chase you   sometimes you let me catch you   now what do I do
it must be funny   you have a wonderful smile   once you were naughty
the holy body   no ▮ come here ▮ do what you want   emerged unscalded

a story framework   extruded by emotion   yes I was ashamed
when they cut the grass   they left a big bunch undone   because of flowers?
no they were just late   perfectly indifferent   so's the chicory
it's all mechanics   it *feels* like love we *act* nice   we're just asteroids
at least that's one view   we're chemically driven   sunflowers by sun
I like ideas   I'll call this *allegory*   it's a pretty name
it never wilts, man!   I was bored: no one chased me   learned a few hitches

I hate to spring it   learned to hang a bear bag high   rid myself of rage
stuff, vehement stuff   4th grade's when it fell apart   gender demonics
I'm too delicate   (: don't be too introspective)   I'm gruff as a man
she sang a high note   she held it like a gold crown   I feel it hurt me
she held long and strong   ending a song of beauty   beauty long and gone

Had better be good

had better be good   the thing about what's holy   caused by mites and mold
I'm playing too rough   the cleanest aquarium   new Chinese lantern
I mean Japanese   read *Asian Art and Culture*   see who learned what when
I knew Father Flye   old, medium height, thin, frail   he was thought special
someone said holy   he bicycled with Agee   in France and England

I didn't know that   can bicycles be holy   yes if all things are
it was the Twenties   they must have seen battlefields   I'm more awake now
the roads not so good   the hazards not so many   harder to pedal
as for what's holy   dead swallowtail on the road   she carried it home
she wants our wishbones   making a dress of wishbones   bones must be holy
but my cold isn't   I could change my thinking here   my woodworking work
nothing but trouble   he imported ideas   holy schematics

I was acolyte   got to lead the procession   bearing the tall cross
Father Flye was there   once he offered Communion   do I remember
he gave a sermon   maybe just read the Scripture   he read the Scripture
held out the platen   everything quavering   just a back-up priest
still could walk and talk   his smile was encouraging   the altar holy

Difference between

difference between   it goes on and it goes on   indefinitely
a clover flower   conic effusion and love   nibbled at by cows
let's say I'm dying   this my final heroics   or calm the terror
dally like others   get your daily double here   duly named doily
a dull sad dolly   sliced dill drilled by hard spit drool   there are examples

difference between   several glyphs in columns   meant a hospital
and the corner ledge   with a wild geranium   woolly with volume
provoked me loosely   you'll never convince me of   you must be kidding
I'm on a sand wedge   but sand and ball will miss me   I'm like a small bat
amazingly small   please, please, no humor ♥ lemurs   (I don't make it out
do you? is it good?)   O Typee your waterfalls   a goat's worth of cheese
(not a club, a *bat*)   she thinks she wants to keep bats   I think they're smelly

difference between   writing and reading it and   writing without that
can't speak up for her   'cause you're kin, others will think   really insincere
the radio says   grippingly self-evident   that's what I'm wishing
a child and now screams   yesterday a dog died there   blind curve on back road
or I just heard blues   a man practicing his drums   not doing ♥ justice

So then it's open

so then it's open   always a moral failure   a thinking fruitcake
some *tertium quid*   you wanted to be with me   what is that plant called
in the space we have   blew ashes off the table   why is the child bored
ran down the cinders   there's a master narrative   the rest of the time
ran down the steep sides   comfortable where he is   so now it's closed up

when the sun goes down   I'm a desert animal   my place in the scheme
is the point how now   no we don't visit enough   *Vista!* Dad would say
big blue Roadmaster   then a big green one with air   a sudden shrinking
why can't I recall   Arundelian marbles   not *aruncula*?
large cardboard cut-out   the Parian chronicles   inscribed on Paros
going really slow   lacked the will for marketing   some keys are shiny
survives as a doll   there's a reason I'm open   a reason I'm closed

not arugula   knowing something for certain   lovable uncle
perfunctory shake   guard at the perimeter   missed the Olympics
platform and barbed wire   the most pitiful gesture   used a gun or knife
had to shoot the deer   I ate the thrushes he killed   but not the goat brains
cows tear grass firmly   I'm afraid I seem furtive   hurled spears over hills

Let's think about this

let's think about this   one, Gerhard, his twin, Hartmut   we walked in forests
visiting fine baths   should we read *Les Miserables*?   in Spanish, *hablo*
is two syllables   I guess *miserables* is three   but would a Frenchman?
some imperfection   think of it as a proud flaw   against pride: still proud
you know, Asian pots   not too hot for summertime   deliberate botch

wore *Lederhosen*   showed off their gymnastic stuff   I'm a manatee
evening laces   you never told anyone   climbed in a window
imagine fainting   get a mucus condition   you see the bottom
we're still taking sides   lecithin as medicine   looks very peaceful
a slippery climb   taking the sides carefully   I'm going to swim
huge koi, some of them   came up to me with whiskers   a private escort
she sure looks pretty   I'm sorry about your mouth   what you had to say

some imperfection?   punched each other and tore hair   goddamn hell broke loose
please just sing to me   she tapped at the vibraphone   wearing real leather
takes a second skin   suggests the inner cosmos   find a healthfood store
country therapy   okay to be so homely   had a huge resolve
an Eskimo Pie   I'm going to have a sundae   who ate the whole box

Following it up

following it up   not like a wagon a mule   looked everywhere
stupid battalions   immediately after   frogs and mice they eat
mini-sentences   we liked the Pret à Manger   eaten handsomely
do you think this queer?   I wore a too-tight caftan   paid for it in cash
sucked the taboo hard   *if he wanted to beat me   I let him beat me*

by now he's long dead   or famous in his circle   unaccounted for
that's not what I want   lunch was food but no soda   does the machine work?
layers of cut grass   dreams getting more slippery   sequestered one's trumps
layers of seaweed   ruined medieval houses   spun out like candy
free cake in layers   remember at McConnell   pilots' training films?
flight simulators?   touching down then taking off   might have to do it
conditions of war   I was a parasite so   I couldn't save her

a nervous old bird   keeping my eye on the nest   coming down through clouds
each twig shines distinct   fire in the forest below   cliff-jut ledge-nest safe
time for a whirlpool   in the Pyrenees she said   bragged like a biker
oh yes my nephew this   my nephew that and my dad   time for a potlatch
suppose you had to   could choose language and country   but must be human

The Serengeti

the Serengeti   the time of year when it rains   new marshes, no moon
the Cape of Good Hope   close to penguins and monkeys   wildly flowering
yellow, & purple   we could go to Hawaii   might not be welcome
we could visit Rome   we'd surely be welcome there   the Pope is funny
you might like Tokyo   I'm hunting for hearth and home   but it's too toxic

to play the next game   ("Geography") you have to   know how things are spelled
if I say *New York*   you'd say *Kingston* or *Kansas*   I'd say *Nome* or *Seoul*
to play "History"   if I said *Renaissance* would   you say *Erasmus*?
or *Erin go bragh*   maybe the *Erie Canal*   it's the same game just
more ethereal   but not so wild as "Ethics"   or "Philosophy"
so open-ended   as "Society" — or "Thought"   — or "Existence," say
which still's not the worst —   being "Language," totally   inclusive and dull

please don't get worn out   they make malts somewhere downtown   images in love
I used her services   not all of them but I was poor   hormones on the street
whips in one window   lady in red, black thigh boots   stage dominatrix
a sheepish sailor   nonetheless went in her door   she pulled her blinds down
Hamburg's Reeperbahn   we're so cosmopolitan   unsafe to forgive

Fix the screen angle

fix the screen angle   report on the platypus   so many wheezes
in the Andes, yes   Peru, yes, Bolivia   so much has occurred
facts versus beliefs   you must relax even more   okay, test your pulse
mint by the mail-slot   merely altitude speaking   if flesh can't matter
S. K. is quoted: "the dead weigh so little." but   their bodies weigh lots

you meant, your letter   news of a health supplement   the immune something
forgetting to plant   invaluable advice   I'm off to walk now
imagine mountains   big mammals surviving there   bears digging in rot
afraid, like rabbits   explains why we have novels   maps & first aid kits
surfed through the traffic   *Look at him! Will he be safe?*   indubitably
screw-like flying thing   intention to make progress   one step then just hope
looks like solid ground   but you're so intuitive   maybe it avoids

your little laptop   tricky in the light of light   hosanna uproar
it was her climax   as a blurb it sold thousands   name your industry
artists are playful   what an excluded middle   lunch-counter romance
not a full circle   like a tricky screen-angle   never start over
absent regretters   we're so fully free to leave   each line a bridge-rail

A more perfect form

a more perfect form   enabling a better love   genetic kind of
I could build a bench   we can all milk cows it's fun   smack flies with BBs
lost your avalanche   fine superiority   in my prayers all night
shopping for a ring   a couple of backpackers   jewelled *rue* of gold
a ring's a torus   no no not usually   nor Moebius strip

fingergrease and wear   is this what I came here for   painting doves for peace
resembles earthquakes   there's room for us to do this   two thousand square feet
bought a copper throne   your friend will do anything   liar's tragedy
I'll be too graceful   says zippers are hard to sew   had the tent repaired
a little water   not to be mechanical   star-struck suppose me
he hopped in his truck   it was a timed exercise   *a near-perfect term*

why so many A's   threat of face on a burner   electric you know
and broke through boxwood   they had a reason he said   lost a second wife
quit their jobs early   to tree-farm, with loblollies   genial people
suppose a merger   all that financial info   a terror in town
all the groundwork done   soon you'll hear the praise of love   iambic donuts

Swerving brilliance

swerving brilliance   of all the things of all of   there's an animal
wondering around   noise of the pet weed-whacker   served little jellies
big-busted cognacs   I'm going unrepressed now   hardly started to
to crow cardinals   very genuine boxers   honored by brand name
honored his typos   removed blemish of his face   ascertained season

to be about to   it may not mean anything   unless you know *Dahl*
botanist who made   who's given credit for them   he said, dahlias
you've got to wonder: *Begon*? and *Zinn*? the system   transparent stuff leaked
took a rough rake to   well my Kleenex box vanished   when she closed the door
whoops! you're such a tease!   they all owned black one-pieces   bank-perfunctory
chaotic bye-byes   if you ever need apples   I *love* your apples
split-pea would be some   truly, sinking like a rock   got your car packed up

points are lost on me   I'm feeling very sad now   slumped by the slo-mo
she has nice earrings   I used to think I was smart   huge planes are circling
will you ever land?   I know there will be a quiz   do *rye* and *wry* count?
haven't heard my horse   a bumpy stark skedaddled   you're out of your *monde*
the last thing he saw   saved out a Mr. Goodbar   stood up and bowed down

Way way too sincere

way way too sincere   where was constant colloquy   of how to address
she's my trophy wife   that was her line   boy do I ☆ miss her   relentless
mi casa es su casa   a web of *non sequitur*   oh please not so think
I'm getting in touch   with expensive therapy   with a black moment
can't abide dingbats   now see what progress you've made   a graceful downfall

easily reviewed   best were challenged, worst were fooled   go ahead, use it
when may I come home   worried about this Asian   culture atmosphere
lingering effects   my metal cup has a ding ☆   bats beside us here
hippie-go-loony   it's anxieties, I guess   ideas denied
like on the code sheet   obsessive-compulsive or   or two-eighty-nine
keeps skipping pages   come here you dismal puppy   would you barbecue?
only one thing worse   if I can just do this fast   it's called a s p a c e bar

take a siesta   go on that's a compliment   I need chickencoops
a huge egg on shelf   far bigger in the story   *we're like, who laid what?*
mellow goldenrod   please take this back to your room   please feed her gerbil
would you like a snake?   please feed your snake her gerbil   late night swim party
cross *Emma* off list   write old what's-his-name a note   *Captain, my Captain*

THREE

Easy for Shakespeare

easy for Shakespeare   simple as pie for Milton   cinchy for Chaucer
not taxing for Pope   like licking sweets for Wordsworth   like eating for Blake
a breeze for Marvell   comforting for Dickinson   no trouble for Pound
no problem for Yeats   so effortless for Wyatt   like breathing for Donne
no pain for Whitman   pretty cushy for Williams   straightforward for Keats

it wasn't for me   that's why I got to do it   flying my own flag
taking the long view   hey! I found a treat, foil-wrapped   get him OFF that stuff
her diaper's soggy   a simple wave/misconstrued   but clearly a sign
a flute, and a song   air, music, a wedding dance   *contemporary*
knee-length and floral   stark, spartan, plain, and true-false   I told you he'd come
inside's a giant   to get him awake's my goal   these yipping voices
to well-wright a wain   where a wain is a wagon   to wright is to make

nice weather I guess   caught your death of cold, have you?   big burly elbows
come down from the hills   he's so large he's too confused   we'll try firecrackers
you like ideas?   go on, tell her about him   I'm not concealing
yes you are you are   otherwise you'd let me go   oranges] [segments
dressed up for dinner   can't stand on his own two feet   drank lots of water

Ran across the street

ran across the street   over there they loved me too   they loved lots of us
I was in London   in the Underground with mice   old-metal colored
a wink example   cough cough harangue cough up cough   nothing's just for show
she's really pushing   always at the edge the weak   the edge is crumbling
boundaries up-whirl   not to say I'm proposing   I mean not am have

a crack in my floor   a notch lost by my window   squared up swung and missed
surrounded by books   mustn't call them works they're texts   no evidence of
found a lucky star   in the tidal pool with crabs   stringy green seaweeds
I was in Berlin   they peed on the monuments   Frau Peukert grew MAD
in indifference   creeping along balconies   pyrotechnical
effusion of love   you know the creamy white stuff   my book's about gifts
MAD's a magazine   he was called a grave robber   a stack of pennies

rather a limp stack   silly to have those pictures   ate an apricot
tomorrow's moon since   I can't say about the moon   our strongest pincers
a vision of words   just growing in space right here   emergent signal
harsh having laughter   I've been made so much fun of   a pre-set diction
previously flown   I couldn't get all the dirt   go on have a drink

What would touching be

what would touching be   rabbits getting their teeth down   embrace in anger
these were my three hugs   Rosa without shyness kissed   Jane was distracted
Karen got flustered   her glasses fell between us   but all three were sweet
too bad they all left   the lives of others are like   unfinished events
swept into story   evil self-aggrandizement   squirted my water

resounding moaners   those two sisters long ago   chicory blueness
I'm fading ta-ta   exercising will teach you   but he's good at golf
pretty soon rabbits   if I can't subordinate   will you ever see
I could go quite blind   maybe it won't matter much   it's so familiar
they're new black walnuts   don't call them old chestnuts, friends   implied a navy
you know, his BIG STICK?   where now is San Ysidro?   the red rock drivel
I can't accept that   go far to be a meanie   strike/was struck/stricken

I've girded my loins   did you notice the effort?   banging on a door
a very small door   it grows smaller with weeping   it's weeped all away
perhaps one lives there   one or two, a few rhinos   dusty thick-skinned beasts
like hippos really   horserivers (skilled in Latin)   don't ask, project it
going out tonight   you're most sweetly demonic   I mean harmonic

Is impossible

is impossible   leaving such small hints for hope   then covering them
seeming to cover   yes happy reading Byron   passion versus rules
down with stupid rules!   suddenly recollecting   to be good at math
someone's being pinched   you have to know I'm failing   don't you feel better?
my red bandanna   crumpled like a mountain now   look! I see cougar!

is impossible   anyway just a boulder   faintest of musics
you *should* climb mountains   not that you must if maybe   you like sea instead
don't try climbing seas   pish you're criminally wacked   big sad rocks for friends
found out my profile   whipped a thing out against me   I juggled their rocks
my name is Gudrun   I know there's sweet about you   you keep cords around
whinnying dreamlife   always room for a story   I'll keep a space free
gripped a gutter spike   designed the box a little   a slightly bigger

coffin's better than   you know: had to cut something   it's Irish bagpipes
blanket of crickets   developed tongue for scallops   mom's cooking tidbits
no I'm not Gudrun   it's shocking you should think so   much about yourself
ask me for a knife   monks descending in baskets   he wore a harness
he wore a helmet   he never needed either   a white bell flower

Her new Miata

her new Miata   it is all given away   asparagus plum
cherry red of course   it is all given away   it never occurred
handles like a dream   it is all given away   images of war-torn
body beautiful   it is all given away   reciting mantra
peace be with you all   it is all given away   peace be with you all

I'm always agon   instead of writing poems   it met the sweet spot
quicksand jungle heat   half a body here and dogs   image of ant head
super colossal   a spring reached through my jeans shorts   never owned pet snakes
she's pretty good at   she suckled him the last time   a fireplace a flare
dazzling slot machines   used to use silver dollars   got back to channel
more big water flume   computer secret kerchief   I said back paddle
I said behemoth   shot that poor huge animal   for out-of-placeness

gave it all away   smashed what was unfixable   not resorting to
sounds like a freight train   it was a train, the 4:10   tingled her nipples
who's not a machine   revenants and butterflies   handles by flitting
leg will fall asleep   getting ready to portage   see the warning signs
edge over now, now   so close to being folly   fine mist in sunlight

Have a nice weekend

have a nice weekend   said the state store employee   grinning sinister
standing tall she was   smiling ridiculously   lips a little slip
you are familiar   you've never heard a cock crow   a bouncing betty
you ate me alive   I had to crawl under stones   we grew like comets
our tails and fireworks   don't expect me to mention   he's not finding cliffs

cliffs swarmed in on him   I like my new wool hatbrim   no golf even once
an opening gush   stark interpenetration   took out the windows
replaced weather wings   sipping it from whence it came   mouth ripped by its force
no automatic   Baxter objected to it   down Baxter good boy
we're not machines yet   machine-like mirrorings yes   she wrote of rivers
and so my *padron*   started thinking racially   shuttered it within
about Cassandra   the chorus of Aeschylus   complains as follows:

You make music that's   a mixture/ugly cries of   terror and high-pitched
melodies. but this   I've stolen it from a book   Susan Griffin's book
but it's how I feel   if you will assume I feel   I'm going wheeling
was a full weekend   first there was Saturday then   plus I had peanuts
by the VCR   ate chips drank a microbrew   renting wilderness

Single lane ahead

single lane ahead   given up within poppies   you must share with deer
better check your tank   I guess I must have cleaned it   in touch with my rage
cleaned his clock with it   what mighty machinist's arms!   sweating on us all
final detainments   soon all you need will surface   bunches of lake stuff
he swam to the dam   when he stopped first at the float   his driving's improved

All you need is love   was James Bond ever humbled?   received your last check
was so glad to see   a single malt from Islay   impeccably dressed
never no never   I read my secret message   I've got my prom dress
shot from a shelter   shot from a blind, an ambush   they fell like dead ducks
I'm here to soothe you   can we afford a massage?   telephoned desire
not 1-900   desire on the fruited plain   air reconnaissance
never had a drink   never denied anything   never told the truth

the corner deli   G and 22nd Street   tied to location
ordered bibim-bab   I'm just guessing Korean   little happy fish
new clean tank gravel   purring *spuff* of the filter   easy now she's sick
in an ambulance   from one scene rushing to one   coiled belts on a shelf
really: and: truly: ridiculous: destiny: saw Parliament vote

Quite a country road

quite a country road   bled the new historicism   got a loo, blank look
happy to take note   it was a big buck with points   mossy and pretty
outside the "clean room"   he now has a desk and chair   followed a career
inner eye at peace   anesthetized, lids held down   discussed a Jewish
it was thought cheating   just about ready to win   carrying a log

ranks a publican   a place to write and a pen   tired of you you snoots
still drives a taxi   had sardines at the Eagle   a sweet symmetry
the flavor was thyme   I mean, the added flavor   a bar showing films
racy and raunchy   our friend Charlie Mannequin   got to prime these now
the road quit no sign   what could I have been thinking   it was so humid
Really. You're bright, eh?   the apse, the nave, in the choir   clerestories around
marvelling beauties   couldn't think about dreaming   owed at least two thou

prudence will dictate   they make fun of how I talk   all my paperbacks
the front covers curl   a big fish at Thrasher's Lake   going surfing now
tornadoed locals   totally insensitive   a cooler came on
something is awake   *thermostat* stands for something   very much plugged in
hard-wired you could say   my novel stayed up too late   bragging on itself

Quiet country road

quiet country road   you're a day-glo tornado   a bit out of place
feathers grew on me   and otherwise estrangement   such a webbiness
are Beefeaters scolds?   tabulating a column   speech as conclusion
a wiry series   function of n-thing equals   those ugly jewels!
who'd want to live there?   I'm glad she said what she did   reclaim the Blew Ridge

a creek with no name   can it be Tough Donny Brook?   it can't be Bull Run
it's Concrete Ditch Run   look at the cat skeleton   pure fear, pure flounder
Sheryl remembered   my being incurable   we might have married
we might have roped steers   I had a hammer, she had   a hard coconut
we watched Superman   in her Wichita rec room   we gee that's touching
my dump truck's air draft   the bicycles all wobbled   the jar has a lid
wincing but convinced   the read-out is still murky   threw candy wrapper

victory dancing   an occasion for getting   a) dressed up b) drunk
c) human contact   let's not get begrudging now   you do look sexy
you can't deny it   with her skirts she made a bed   barnstorming came back
amyl nitrate the   little capsule stuff to smell   and then laughing gas
hard to be Roman   all these fine Greek hedonists   water siphoning

Mr. Jefferson

Mr. Jefferson   we read for Mr. Mader's   and what he would do
(Mr. Jefferson)   was read what things he wanted;   when he'd feel like it
he'd find a new one   so he'd have 18 books out   spread over his floor
oh they were big books   leatherbound they'd stay open   he'd stretch out and read
a personal trick   like JFK, speed reading   they gave us machines

a clipboard-sized box   fit down over some text page   and a sliding bar
speed you adjusted   I once got to a thousand   I'm slowpokey now
not my mother though   in the old silent movies   she'd be embarrassed
read the captions fast   always first but unable   to stop laughing first
I like a slow text   so every text seems slow   Heaney's <u>Sweeney</u> or
Jameson's big opus   now I'm sure Byron loved her   a gift's a good thing
Becky for instance   she gave me a book on gifts   what I'll give her back

more than jam you know   more than a dictionary   such an interrupt
I'm sure it's pleasing   I threw all those rules away   used my story box
don't usually   still quite puzzled about Bec   reciprocity
don't worry I will   have to go beyond the lines   terrible dangers
those squeaks and chirrups   it might almost be a game   let's see how to play

Argued about points

argued about points   almost reached a certainty   retied my laces
ran a quarter mile   what would *respectable* mean?   removed my t-shirt
threw water balloons   all around it's summertime   frogs by the water
where frogs go snakes go   busses meaning business   transport policy
we've been transported   why should there be policies?   we loved what it was

full of questionnaires   our doorbell never so rung   our dog so hyper
Down, Hyperpuppy!   the willow: ask about it   or the copper beech
72 points   approximately an inch   nyah nyah told you so
you'd have me confused   my agreeability   DAMAGED MY MANHOOD
microdramatics   fueled by industrial   you know, snoops and spooks
it'll be sadness   think of this as the last time   wait a second you
tent caterpillars   there needs to be a fungus   okay, you be cool

forever mindful   delete *forever*; use *un-*   don't unmindful me
had great telescopes   I've met some slippery elms   went to kabuki
I'd love to fit in   unless you've got a pocket   we use huge trash bags
darling I mean huge   easy big enough for you   no big as you are
let's be more cheerful   campers I'm proud of your spunk   I think I meant that

Screwed up the contract

screwed up the contract   not joint custody at all   which film should we see
just enough constraint   it's all I've ever wanted   slammed a mosquito
bring the ball wag wag   it's not me it's an army   starring Belmondo
many cheerfully   what are these pitiful bugs   their lives for a cause
marriage tents to be   indifferent to sin tax   I'm German enough

a sultry sparkle   it should underline your breast   oh I didn't aim
a horn I like horn   elegance in fairy rings   not a mosquito
smashed onto the pad   nonetheless smashed, cousins too   stuff on my glasses
gray Baptist church van   country people do health stuff   ditto junk food stuff
I've gone 40 now   helmet meets air and makes noise   20's okay too
I was upside down   feathery with stuff hanging   you could have crushed me
please try to like this   idea of a grimace   choral remarking

don't cut yourself off   I'm the youthful Houdini   I'm the strong man gone
you're the singing air   recall that wild taverna   not the pure calm night
oh but pure and calm   I sing like a mournful moth   see my air's not on
sheer plod, stick to me   it may be only fringes   or unwoven threads
making magic here   a frail fabric of seeming   seeming a fabric

This might disgust you

this might disgust you   watching a starling waddle   hunched over his sex
a needed ugly   history of sailing ships   your clipped collection
in time go backwards   open your mouth obvious   later sweating it
from this human milk   light sleeping nights by traffic   needled it deeply
I've struck a discord   I've struck goo and cried freely   I've struck a liar

that birdie's flown off   mentioned moons in the city   an hibernal doom
pretty violence   looking back at the future   bore their quadruplets
to distinguish us   our catalog of courses   that whumping frenzy
today's trip Motown   Mom says plantar fascitis   Mom uses words well
getting over it   she worked as a water witch   and the IRS
took her tool cost off   severely inferential   intrinsic apple
Wham-O or Speedo   Mickey Mouse spinning a top   a long white string frapped

scarred a piano   herd a cow, a herd of yaks   Tibetan cowpokes
acquired overbite   for a quarter you can see   Ralph loves me me me
putting puttees down   becoming otherworldly   limp oak leaf sinking
please clean my fountain   these doggy decaying things   that's an old CD
a place to junk stuff   on Second or Third they sell   (fences) stolen bikes

Today August 6

today August 6   51 years after it   and I'm still 50
I taught a student   20 years old I suppose   from Hiroshima
earlier this year   there's good news there and sadness   not included here
in fairness to that   there's no fairness probable   I'm letting bells ring
turned off my alarm   did laundry early so that   we all stayed balanced

not included here   the newsreel pictures in school   webbing to nightmare
whose resolution   it might be time to buy socks   due to paradox
Marx, yes, overdue   you might check the shelf again   please don't forget me
commodificate   *etched shadows on building walls*   lamp posts or humans
humans and posts gone   long people to pilgrimage   disturbed by disrupt
shrimping industry   climbing a mountain these thoughts   an old feed store hat
stumbled in chiggers   burned till warped then burned some more   little ugliness

from Hiroshima   bungled honor retrieval   ate humor as work
meaning newspapers   quick the latest debacle   *a drowsy numbness*
won't go down farther   scratched it gently but it bled   why these skin problems
learned to spit harder   not the nicest kind of friends   nicest kind of friends
they'll tell you you're wrong   you might be dead when they're done   — 1945 —

Rounded up sandals

rounded up sandals   about time — summer's ending   ahead what a blur
tired of politics   all the gibbons do is howl   "I" don't "mean," *really*
you switched cars again   I paid for a quick truing   annual stickers
oh that is stupid   it's so easy to erase   you'll never ever
delete most of it   like rejuvenating lawns   with plugs of good grass

do you know how hard   she was working at her work   until she couldn't
then a blip imaged   maybe it wasn't cancer   the way people talked
she just disappeared   toucan-handled umbrella   mighty artistic
I'd want flamingo   speaking of lawn ornaments   a stack of cupids
notched one on his gun   a primer of lyric forms   most insipid soup
weaned well at 13   those people they were just here   I'm starting to boil
défense de fumer   you must love your Latin roots   *meringue, cha-cha*

to become Sir Jacques   no, *mon chevalier* perhaps   surely not Saint Jacques
we ate *croques monsieurs*   I mean that grilled cheese thingie   before microwaves
it's going to rain   the joke is they don't have teeth   she won't chew it off
threw down decorum   short narrow stairs in the stacks   we touch in passing
white coffee to go   got the car, the dog to go   we're with visitors

Yellow flyswatter

yellow flyswatter   we've had experiences   we were buttonholed
we were upended   we never met a man we   it was all girls there
we ate long thin breads   at first hard but soft when boiled   Noodle Mania!
those were real magpies   he should see me now I'm bald   he'd ask, "SO AM I
THE BEST ONE EVER?"   I'd say no I've had better   professor who flirts

absent in the mall   exit by the Red Lobster   look for Toys 'R Us
Staples is below   America uniformed   what's wrong, precisely?
if you need paper   better find a paper store   made fun of this how
borrowed a huge wave   you know there's a sauna here   just peel that apart
you're charitable   always you had a nice streak   suffered blunt trauma
no, trauma for sure   the hot sand like spikes or knives   the worst was next up
hey my man got rich   someone's touching the low rocks   I'm tracing hearts here

someone's touching leaves   yellow leaves fallen early   forming coronals
in the stacks reading   finding sensibilities   planning an immense
the oildrum if clean   taught me several love quirks   except for touching
touched in algebra   picked wild watercress to soup   such a sweet slight stream
then forget-me-nots   declined in its forgiveness   forgot my finger

Somersaults in love

somersaults in love   anvil-headed thunderclouds   flakes drifting about
ceiling paint's come loose   above my weak eyes' threshold   just twisting like weeds
Crazy Legs Leonard   couldn't replicate the scheme   went back to water
went back to thatched huts   went alone nary a friend   preset to catch me
circulated through   succotash is nourishing   volumes of gravy

loved your Melville book   squished me for being happy   said I made it up
loved that Freud-Jung thing   we must have watched the Lakers   the Milwaukee ones
or Minnesota   puh-leez don't expect me to   Mahler Juicy-Fruit
I had a biplane   I flew to Argentina   why make us be sad
you know the buildings   just like normal folks' buildings   never yet had fleas
stylish to cry here   along the road built cry points   hard to disguise it
there aren't any more   he wrote a hundred or so   by sweet Lodore Falls

I'm kind of picky   grew okra better each year   communicated
Pooh butter that's fun   bump the bums at Leicester Square   a bit bigoted
a bit revanchist   picked what for jam that one year   found a tarnished bell
Good night! Sweep it up!   as a percent, not really   looked just like Grandma
you would never dare   I'm going to get stubborn   windlasses working

FOUR

She had a vision

she had a vision not delicate but lovely in its crazy way:
she'd come to D.C. sneak past the guarded entrance (maybe too easy)
leaping, scale the fence cross the moat and meet tigers her death in their mouths
she was a poet of a kind, as imagined poets seem to be,
and swam, I'm guessing as all must in such waters and is now quite dead

totally gruesome and time's up: put her back down gently as you can
the *Post* was bothered *improve the security* *if she'd been locked up*
(don't take me for true) but lots of people felt that (do me a favor:
find me a lawyer if the *Post* takes exception: a really good one)
lots of people sue for all I know this crazy poet woman sued
sued left and sued right broke and miserable and no kind of friend left
maybe she caused it caused each ounce of pain she felt I vilify her

I'm not relenting: if she caused her own pain she (sorry) deserved it
if she sued people if she hid in the fringes being so angry
I'm fine about her she got just what she wanted those huge teeth so strong
her little arms and waist her neck cracking like a stick her fresh gooey blood
the tender bowels and inside her puny ribs that stupefied heart

Wiggled her trinkets

wiggled her trinkets   half the market rapturous   springtime belly girl
with narrowing eyes   invented the promenade   got my approval
joy that day in mud   risking our Bible studies   hewed the shiny ones
yes I signed for it   played late night Pictionary   lots to disperse towards
could have played Jotto   his phone call unexpected   a cracked, slanted floor

they will always play   Grace observed before she died   wherever they are
but then aren't kids long   but then when's the movie start   but *then*'s the moment
knew some precursors   zero-based my budgeting   I want wads of bills
couldn't find their graves   confused the cemetery   crapped-out old keyboard
a town near Neptune   never met a soul from there   don't meet one like me
his hand on his neck   it's so hard to count people   my subjects the frogs
a box for a nose   kleenex and a runny nose   pretty state park beach

because a fire sale   admittedly generous   mishandle her test
wrong wrong wrong you're wrong   a game-playing family   she seemed unpregnant
watched Nerf basketball   watched underwater polo   testing the TV
jacked up her rhythm   speeding down the Interstate   needles quivering
not outrunning it   tried using cunning, tried luck,   windfall, waterfall

If there were others

if there were others   already spoken proving   touring Nottingham
no Robin Hood stuff   strict historical you see   they should let us in
hammer up some signs   but it's a different way   they let you smoke here
I never touched them   I was too young they were dead   one so already
one soon enough so   guessing that you understand   trying to make light

without making fun   climbed the stile but kicked her jaw   seek adjustables
drew the first stapler   please God such a one is rich   nervous hammering
he's still practicing   purpled by aggravation   stepped in took over
now the ground is flat   chopped and filled a big roadway   lost a lot of dough
DNA-type work   from forgery detection   create a board game
some of you collect   some are duped and need experts   an expert gets rich
at least makes enough   can pay back those college loans   broke her neck sharply

her bumper's layered   sticker on top of sticker   mine says Brake For Moose
It Could Save Your Life   picked that up in New Hampshire   kind of faded now
kind of silly now   returned his clean underwear   communal washers
someone's teakettle   turned on a precondition   *selva oscura*
sure there were rabbits   it's not what counted the most   the mirror hit her

Do work on your time

do work on your time   why would you tidy up now   as an example
as a reminder   before drowsing sweeps through you   a party to this
and jelly donuts   not responsible for her   pointing to body
could use a nice trim   my problem with your essay   what's on the pool floor?
recovered logics   ruled his every action   we've eroded more

punched the button in   *Star Dust* sort of like "star stuff"   skyline lost in clouds
my hand's fault, I guess   tired of it being pretty   tired being pretty
that's just pitiful   a blister being chosen   it shows a bored Mars
the planet of course   Jupiter has stomachaches   Saturn's hung over
the cartoons had this   Pluto is constipated   Earth must have asthma
room of dead rich men   for days now the flies have worked   shoplifted oatmeal
the bottom opens   freefall all over again   horses and reindeer

from radiation   the more you wince the wiser   explain tips as gifts
in the tank goo-goo   *ich hab' kein Geld* to give you   I became stable
horribly tortured   a slideshow without story   some are in backwards
some are upside-down   factories daisies weddings   sounds like you were there
goaded and stabbed at   having to flee, fleeing, gone   stones lying in dust

For tonight's dessert

for tonight's dessert   you can't fake disjointedness   escorted limos
Hey Sport, long time, hey   coming home from Africa   20,000 miles
they add half again   I give him my flyer miles   my brother why not
fields of sunflowers   osprey on nesting platform   that Chestertown day
a good bounding line   Blake liked a good bounding line   and "Boy," Chesterton

the kitchen polite   what is stainless has been scrubbed   look at that jacket
a soldier shot him   the ricochet afterward   hit the soldier's knee
they say when he talked   he was that kind of speaker   you didn't know it
still he made you cry   not knowing it you still cried   that was how he spoke
they say they all cried   none of them noticed a thing   their faces still wet
at night when he quit   they'd turn to hug their neighbors   all their shirts were wet
they'd look at themselves   they couldn't understand it   —My brother, why not?

a whole cult of mags   screw in to tighten focus   it's short for something
bloomed this time last year   the desperate swallowtails   having happy hour
puckered up to learn   became a *fusty old nut*   not yet sincerely
triumphal arches   aqueducts and hippodromes   roads and circuses
villa at Capri   villa anywhere will do   *runs through the sword; dies*

It's becoming clear

it's becoming clear   I laid out a bunch of track   whoa! cities sprang up
who are palookas   in their being essential   filled with sweet liquor
false fronts from hurt eyes   it was difficult driving   after such concern
not by conference   it was all coming from ghosts   Jersey a county
not by competence   in her rear view mirror seen   drumming partridges

heard special remnants   the great balustrades of moon   little light flounces
the secrets drifting   canoe tied under a tree   so wanting pretty
making wax clearer   deep in molecular night   redemptiveness as
hogbitten diehards   pluralized meaning others   now shuffle tap slide
made his cat money   don't you like/Garfield's big/smile   it's like SO toothy
into money, yes   Paul did something with Jesus   not commercially
all that came later   trust me, I'll keep track of things   (we went to THE track)

a salaried mess   chucked it; sparked up a typhoon   jitters ♥ by jeepers
went south, I've heard said   used to be a fox lived here   yes, right where we are
exasperate you?   *you're* exasperating *me*   *used* to be a fox
once they reduce us   first they'll try with knock-out mice   so they took his bike
quoting me I guess   Fred, I don't know why, but Fred   fit into the scheme

Time to think of fall

time to think of fall   impending as if to say   *why will you do this?*
notebooks and pencils   a graphing calculator   calm those gunboats down
I'm getting more so   you're getting even more so   we've gotten it bad
there's a crazy child   disguised like a black-faced sheep   broken-neck I fear
not glued up exact   if lathe-work, contorted, freaked   spun off and cracked deep

cart-and-pony talk   Samuel Beckett's the man   a touching story
mothered by Scorch-Earth   fathered by Outman-Himself   married to Hard-Board
they're kissing too long   we can't go on till they're back   oh good, now *you* go
spit to grip harder   time to bust your ass with rocks   bulletholes in bars
bit and jumped away   horse named 7-11   acted like a flea
horrible sunburn   from rocky pine to sagebrush   brickmasons' rhythms
I keep telling you   this is going to be hard   I'm open all night

they circled in rings   they hosted a stuff party   entered creamy toasts
dreamed of sunkenness   near-cosmetic consciousness   a friend said "gnarly"
demanded, we guess: interacts with local brains   (similars divorced
(unlikes divorced too   (I'm getting married tonight   (this my bride's present
(you think she'll like it?   [computer-frustrated days   nights of little bugs]

Used to sweeteners

used to sweeteners   because why shouldn't things seem   better to taste buds
it's convenient   using the car for errands   air-conditioned too
packages we buy   special opening methods   just zip, grasp here, pull
to open CDs   to open NutriGrain bars   turkey sandwich meat
to throw things away   plastic liners in trash cans   taking things easy

ho-hum; critique's done   by my watch it's time to play   come sister, you should
I know I'm begging   do this just once more with me   I won't cheat, promise
(Lucy picks ball up   Linus, thrown off, falls backward   every autumn)
oh it's Charlie Brown   some things you don't have to know   astrophysics stuff
beyond the basics   mergers and acquisitions   cream puffs and soufflés
repair of air bags   decorating swizzle sticks   4-color printing
even how to spell   *minuscule* not *miniscule*   those cast-off careers

you didn't see it?   I'll check with the designer   people need warnings
PELIGRO! maybe   don't just leave holes in the road   you're starting to fix
but have to go off   on a toilet break let's say   here she comes dreamy
her new Miata   could do serious damage   be more forgiving
extend your effort   syntax should embrace us all   now, please, can we play

Each phrase a caption

each phrase a caption   hey that's a good idea   this phrase a widget
you don't see of what   but you're in on the in-joke   stop your squabbling now
back to the canoe   a little breeze pushed in through   hostile to what's near
the first thing moving   a dark insect like a fly   first there were roosters
only as far sound   also a chippering bird   several of them

a huge water vat   why not welcome its blueness   big enough for boats
I can't see his whales   his brim lowered till his eyes   a spout from his head
in a speech balloon   everything was written   it looked like clover
leased as cow pasture   it was near Poor House Farm Road   not registered to
went to the court house   needed a building permit   wanted a short stoop
to detect earthquakes   it's a jigsaw confusion   needs clever sewing
always in a rush   ask anyone who knows me   always more sincere

swallowtail flew past   number two of things moving   things I've seen moving
a sudden embrace   you need to squeeze a little   makes it more money
guess we missed the turn   still learning to fly this thing   haven't crashed (not yet)
"you should feel, that's all"   "be nice to understand you"   oh now I feel bad
oh now I feel bad   you've shown me my *Inferno*   I was so comfy

My fiercest lover

my fiercest lover   where can you possibly go   much too all come-on
shameful opening   the point must be to struggle   overcoming shame
not exactly shame   equivalently nervous   worried, elusive
so, bold is perfect   HELLO I'M AN M-9 TANK   then to be nimble
butterfly-catching,   cloud-chasing, wants lemonade   boardwalk ribbon-dance

preliminaries   hot ready to glow again   unmaking himself
unnaming himself   resculpted the old farmlands   thick mist this morning
sun's just area   lightest sector of the white   but his work flecks through
spires as if from space   lodged princely among us then   given by clear light
the usual stuff   noon to two to find meaning   first asked nebula
second asked the elm   but never asked the asker   well maybe sort of
never found solace   wanted you to read my mind   never said it right

was right all along   it's the crackling forest fire   flames taller than trees
flames taller than trees   by now I know what is right   right *les flammes du mal*
then her father died   her body a sign to me   who were all those kids
smaller than real life   we were dolls laughing on shelves   that stopped happening
I did do TM   gentle wavemarks of deceit   smoothing, smothering

My ride had five hills

my ride had five hills   three were really pretty large   I did each one twice
we grew potatoes   fun, potatoes, and okra,   Egyptian onions
she always camped out   3 or 4 weekends a month   to escape the house
all his socks were "greige"   stained maroon by shoe leather   ironed white hankies
she kept a Bible near   her nightgowns were blue, beige, white   with embroidery

someone stole my bike   I kept it on the back porch   all of us were home
she made her own clothes   quilted her own comforter   from butterfly sheets
we played "Flinch" a lot   always that meant we got fudge   in winter, cracked nuts
I built a wood fence   dug holes for 32 posts   Travis helped me out
she played piano   I think she stayed in chorus   she was pretty good
we grew corn and squash   radishes and tomatoes   we made dill pickles
she went to college   she bought a book on Sputnik   an early frisbee

once, the plum had fruit   we got her to make plum jam   sealed with paraffin
he had golf habits   he'd wash his irons with soap   had a ball marker
we drove one Christmas   beyond Oaxaca and back   in our yellow car
she studied Spanish   could read *Las Americas*   loved flowers, star-names
her home was L.A.   she went to UCLA   she moved and we met

Goofy frogs *wonk wonk*

goofy frogs *wonk wonk*   unbrokenness of crickets   mini-sentences
looking into space   many possibilities   really not much else
the Posturepedic   the air on so cold last night   they'd gitched in the box
dooming your dumplings   only the barbecue left   gnus good for carving
haven't scratched it yet   come on over and try it   who's talking and why

who's weeping and why   a mouth shut because because   it won't be the same
worked in her swimsuit   having some kind of something   say some stupid stuff
it needs an oil change   it needs a state inspection   Carl hated such lists
Dickey's laundry list   for example which he thought   Dickey could publish
well where's your rhythm   big boy, what's been biting you   among the short hairs?
pfoo pfoo and pfooey   it begins, "June in Dublin"   *what you got on birth?*
your friend the otter   rises glossy from water   squirmy and other

he left you this note   it's a strict column of ens   *nuptial*? or *NORAD*?
about where I lost   your millenial moment   if that's what you said
I did swat that fly   I'm imagining a day   this one, in the past
it's not been locked up   you may enter the garden   turn right at the bricks
tiptoe to my chair   I'm just past the sundial   please cover my eyes

Giving you reasons

giving you reasons   hardly if I wanted to   like fishing dry ponds
pyramid *del Sol*   of Moon and Feathered Serpent   the great Avenue
clouded mirthlessness   I mean hucksters at the top   not wanting you calm
wanting you angry   buy an orange shut me up   a kind of reason
engaged a poor child   you can't buy a guide to this   you can buy so much

these books I'm reading   some spirit stuff some cynic   let me wash my hands
had to use GoJo   Lemon GoJo gallon jug   because this thick grease
hard work getting smart   better to fly than always   trying to take off
all those rocks around   say the yard's looking better   grass mowed and weeded
dishes washed and dried   keeping us at the ready   media happened
mixed in suddenness   specific occurrences   alloyed partial truths
that is, staged it new   that is, defied a magnet   that's that and now this

had to climb them all   tried to pass it off but choked   gave up and turned back
drew herself as nude   a thigh-banging time of it   sculptural weakness
high above ocean   the bridge blowing and swaying   flung a huge red rake
over the highway   a hangar-like tent miles long   caught on my van's roof
must be a movie   version of the Space Program   people in lab smocks

He fell out of bed

he fell out of bed he does it say twice a week this time it hurt him
old bony body filled a pan with stuff to help caulking gun, washcloth
we liked being there the dog the kids and Kathy along with my folks
while my dad was off fixing his hip or shoulder I danced with my mom
my hand grazed her robe I touched where her legs began and I had come from

it was a moment no one got very flustered the dog stayed asleep
I talked with Andrew we felt sorry for my dad he'd fallen at 4
it did wake me up I didn't know what woke me I got back to sleep
this was in my dream but also it was the truth well part of it was
and there's more to ask why he wanted a flashlight whose old house this was
was breakfast coming who was sizzling that bacon when did I shift out
the aquarium what would make it have come next or then the car dream

I'm feeling good now my daughter my wife my mom my dad, me, my son
the dog still asleep the rest of us united meaning all are one
each is at an age there's reason to dance around sure we're all damaged
the old ones will pass the house is even older beautiful antiques
rich family quilts what the dog is sleeping on forming the focus

A certain rhombus

a certain rhombus   a natural condition   outside gravity
inside a mink coat   grind up the raw furless minks   be food for something
must be the trout farm   they just drain out the water   cull the slimy floor
turns fertilizer   we slip those trout on the grill   not stream-caught maybe
that's the way work works   another kind of circuit   raining to the north

roosting and nursing   replenishment counting toes   re-erects it new
brushed a rubber stuff   just one of the things we do   frenziedly foreign
WHAT seems like nothing?   two difficult sandwiches   sticking those toothpicks
she climbed up Tetons   she must have laughed about it   hauled a piccolo
she wants it to "hum"   I offered to replace it   that gap was too big
on a pogo stick   briefly view geography   stuck the chandelier
white rice cooked: egglike   maternity ideas   all a bit moot moot

I hurt his feelings   two of them hurt his feelings   he'd wanted their hugs
it'll be a book   an 800-page novel   it will need details
here's thinking of one   respondent to the jury   it wasn't Provence
not Provence at all   there was a cave however   huge sad forebodings
a little merlot   nearly bubbly zinfandels   certainly right there

Here now the first time

here now the first time   you're the first who touches me   take me in your hands
if our eyes could meet   but mine would be so *open*   you might not be strong
you need to be strong   strong here & strong now & now   I can't compel you
you need to hear this   these are not preconditions   I'm nothing unless
here again and now   my eyes will never see you   touch, do as you please

your hands soothing me   the tips of your fingers slow   trace my silhouette
addressing each rib   you ignore no inch of me   you've known one like me
you have not known me   this is the first time for me   the first time with you
I am excited   I'm so happy I may laugh   I won't hold it back
I want to be yours   naturally, as I am   if I cry I cry
I cannot tell you   if you want me as I am   it is the first time
touch each inch of me   push against my breathing pulse   there's heat here for you

there's space here for two   I can't tell how but I know   I almost see you
I am so ready   I am ready for you now   this is now here you
I am you feeling   you are feeling all I am   I am all for you
this is the time *this*   what we are making, ourselves   ourselves we are now
and *still* this goes on   maybe you had misgivings   this was a giving

Dropped or forgotten

dropped or forgotten   crushed like a bug on a grille   suddenly vanished
geese checking their lakes   cows sampling the acreage   nervous ants testing
ran today's errands   car passed the state safety check   read the local news
I'm not sure of this   what is "psychic implosion"   open and gulping?
at the dollar store   got mugs with salt shaker tops   small ones for cordials

bought a hacksaw blade   did not want a long gabfest   got barely a smile
oh this is the life   no dropsical dryads here   come here you rummies
she liked Rydal Mount   the croquet lawn talk I gave   yes, on "Daffodils"
that isn't its name   it's what most people call it   it has no title
I wandered lonely   as a cloud is how it starts   you recognize it
published dialogues   *The Nation*, *New Republic*   certainly artful
do you play croquet?   I am the best, you dognose!   sounds like a challenge

what did she look like   I can see her as a girl   kind of mischievous
BRIGHT red hair, freckles   one of those tiny noses   could amuse herself
a strong teenager   tricky about the body   danced all right I bet
church and relatives   in college she must have talked   I can't hear her talk
Mother it's your life   I'm wondering about it   before you knew Dad

FIVE

Kill bugs who irk you

kill bugs who irk you   dig a ditch with a steel spade   sit on bunched moss clumps
erroneousness   infantile misprisioning   nonconformity
oak is a warp of tree   crows can fly high but stay low   you must stew tough meat
braggadocio   pre-Congregationalist   fungibility
tall grass and small worms   paid his tax and got wax back   swam in surf, ate clams

built a gnomic mouse   imbedded answers in it   latent till diseased
wheeled in a circus   of labcoats/with language bursts   previewed the targets
future-focused looks   here's the winkling creature now   this last-month's model
lame and sunken-toothed   shows of cruelty whooping   shade corporeal
my family gauze   a barrier to grief land   voices removing
ringmaster preacher   Bible under the Big Top. . .   no, no, wrong circus
circus of science   attendants trainees and aides   stethoscopes, pencils

well, *the other thing*   *I have been almost able*   *to say* is not here
endless gorging ghosts   I feed them bowls they ask for   you would hesitate
may the dear lord rest   the assembled picturebooks   hey those are pretty
after all I care   after this I may repent   yes, examine me
I will not thwart you   my teaching's *straying from me*   I see the new strain

Ambient data

ambient data   skylight, white noise, jabbering   adjusted therefore
a warm forgiving   versus mere warm tolerance   one got the embrace
two was not kicked out   look I've left the door open   I've put meat scraps out
it's time we were friends   I wait, with heebie-jeebies   who's making noise there
yes in the alley   stop bumping things and come in   you might get clean now

drank coffee with L.   attacked confessionalism   may have attacked her
sorry about that   stars are rare with all these clouds   sunlight melts the mist
candles by the pool   last night's party evidence   where was I and why
no "pop" Heidegger   can't repeat that tone in pop   fire out of control
limit the damage   cut a cordon around it   let it rage within
where was I and why   *thrown* he'd say; what can you do?   such a churchly voice
that's what won't translate   its caustic globalizing   wants everything

flew my red pennon   that means "plotting victory"   it means no such thing
what *is* it with you?   well it was raining, and cold   so I flopped around
they started to laugh   we were all really laughing   we were being there
hey monkey monkey   thrown into such a strange place   get your vests back on
let's paddle some more   how we bailed Heidegger out   and got home OK

Discovered a wall

discovered a wall   fortunately moveable   unfortunately
indestructible   you push on it and it gives   seems to disappear
something else gets blocked   I'm developing a tag   you know tag, good sport
maybe this wall's good   maybe it just wants to play   I've been so earnest
see, voices laughing   I've never heard frogs yelling   a chair to sink in

tell me your secrets   the world already knows them   start thinking kathunk
I'd not have said so   but he was right a nice dress   she changed for dinner
awash in concepts   nice how that macro readies   I'm looking for you
yes, you're lovely, yes   someone sounds like a chipmunk   heavens to velcro
the whelk collection   designed by a committee   looks like a gene job
I tried to sneak off   bruised my chin on that old wall   whose corral is this
I guess I have to   the way my branches mingle   not stopped by the edge

that is not always   such a welcome forgotten   we can start over
I liked his painting   if you had stayed together   I would have bought one
but you are my friend   he's the divorced discarded   and no longer paints
so that means I'm rich   time to take a vacation   time to splash in streams
let water slip by   slipping its tie to its bed   rocketing goodbye

Speared on the parkway

speared on the parkway   pickup straight into a tree   maybe suicide
going 60 or   or 50 and just lost it   solo vehicle
easy stretch of road   cab crunched into humps of mush   ways out of that: nil
the cops waved us by   get on by or be a risk   don't respect the dead
respect the living   I'm not joking there's a fly   I can't quite see it

now the fly is dead   that's what happens when you leave   a big guy alone
who's got a flyswatter   with a big fly all abuzz   I mean a big fly
think of the machines   lined up making flyswatters   our excavations
shovels, cars, ore-trains   the smelting and refining   extruding the wire
shipping then shaping   and to form the plastic head   the diverted oil
precise distilling   additions modulations   forming in the molds
hardening liquid   married to wire handle-form   sold, bought, hung ready

a lot of punch here   that pesky little house fly   on the wrong side of
so *I heard a fly   buzz* and brought my denial   my huge weight to bear
I stalked and waited   and in my dream this morning   I found two lovers
incredibly saved   the cab split in two, they climbed   out with ease and grace
they took a calm stroll   among unsuffering trees   went home like angels

Foot traffic welcome

foot traffic welcome   yes I'll take a hard massage   beautiful bovines
she's waiting for a "click"   as halos signal meaning   we say she needs meat
she needs measurers   he always buys spoons for her   she isn't nearly
it's in the muscles   their beauty is muscular   also skeletal
we're not talking plants   there's another line nearby   to smile satisfied

water mocassin   reached and caught a fish to eat   they studied nature
stranded in rhythms   reading her cost him four days   they could hug later
a timid sergeant   but you, you could say, you could   reduce it to grime
broken ideas   opened geodes with a sledge   and vacuum cleaner
I've kept my wrapper   I've thrown my gum out in it   I've followed orders
we entered the woods   swatting mosquitoes fiercely   did not get to get
lost and abandoned   huge desert above the falls   extended the frame

quoted explicit   images of great power   lovemaking couples
I'm painting over   too purple-flecked with self-doubt   in a case like this
bubble ink-jet smacked   terminological doubt   doubt like a rowboat
it's how you got here   guess you don't have a ski-doo   no waterjetskis
and no QE II   nothing from the Cunard line   swept with a mad joy

Couldn't find the spot

couldn't find the spot   bushwhacking too strenuous   logging road just stops
yes a background noise   it might've been Panther Falls   might've been the wind
found a Coke bottle   a dumptruck load of firewood   *slow fire of* debris
oaks and oak saplings   black ends of down trees orange   with bracket fungi
save it for later   nicer to use cared-for paths   also it's lunchtime

walked around the lake   deer on the grassy pasture   a weird-looking mountain
"skirted" muddy spots   meaning came close, not too close   lazy rain begins
what was your insight   rolled down the whole earthdam slope   *contra naturam*
play over purpose   the dam's important purpose   children speedily
try another thing   scary puppets out of socks   matchbox hamster case
wrapped, aluminum   /baked those taters in the coals   /words that never end
matchbox for coffin   one parakeet named Sandy   a story of apes

heard praise of voodoo   lift your feet and run away   bounced up at the end
hides himself at home   the plot really hasn't changed   now they're going to
that's a chimney tile   made so it won't freeze and crack   not to believe that
distract me within   building models of failures   used a Rube Goldberg
what a cartoonist   drew crazy inventions and   now he's on a stamp

Might be city lights

might be city lights   four or five similar towns   from a mountain rim
the connected towns   snug on low peninsulas   the bays eerie blue
dark flat horizon   only a few lights below   in the dark foreground
a dark serigraph   like art in a motel room   why it's in your life
why's anything there   tell the story of dark light   on the wall it seems

fought off a mourner   took two years of cross-stitching   said she was obsessed
what is pepper spray   fought off attacking mourners   mastiff wanting meat
banged a big blue ball   didn't tell anyone why   took time to come down
sailed like a balloon   sailed like an interruption   changed the flow of things
only trains on tracks   we're getting used to noisy   it's Dylan again
Mr. Tambourine Man   what decade are we in now   age of filigree
punched his ATM   having brushed his hair before   went on tumbling on

toured the wineries   improved their disposition   to admire the world
as if they might buy   when they finally found where   fated to settle
coffee stain I guess   often she humming fragments   his was about time
what a pretty verse!   oh you say that to them all   I might be in love
you can't use that word   reinsert your daytime file   at last we're ready

Prioritizing

prioritizing: before we lay foundation   let's plan for floor drains
one inside, one out   we have to have one outside   for the basement door
the other's extra   often inside stuff's extra   construed as private
in time this will blur   I see myself/cartwheeling   downward battlements
bespoke gracefulness   electronic boomerangs   tries spatter-painting

simultaneous: the way he did his laundry   the way the plot looked
fussed with droopiness   this is very important   try to understand
poodles need those cuts   fur-related skin disease   and sheer beauty of
an idealist   that's me and the rest of you   don't make me say it
nice weather we've got   yes ma'am powerful fine air   care for some sushi?
bunged his shin but laughed   purchased the green supplement   expected results
posted the results   everyone was laughing   you know, Black Elk too

trigonometry: some hatchu got theh pahdner   interfering waves
sure we collect stamps   S & H Green Stamps, food stamps   had a coupon wad
threw out the gum wad   if you don't have 4-wheel drive   went up to the sky
about now they're done   went to the organic store   whence supplements come
a child needs its mom   its mom must be sort of near   near enough to hear

You got your dump truck

you got your dump truck   it's got tons of stuff on it   *there are ways to look*
it may have jewels   depending which stones you want   it may completely
but what a bruiser   humming crud down the highway   compressing bridges
getting that load on   graceful from a distance like   V's airport ballet
useful yes of course   but brute fact canceling that   and what a back draft

then when I saw cows   the whole herd was lying down   getting bathed by rain
grr, Grr, GRR, I said   not even you responded   and now you're asking
why I keep quiet   I live in the preemie ward   I'm a nervous dad
low birth-weight babies   they'll do that to a person   cute unlikely things
probably it's genes   some folks just can't bring the full   rondure stuff out whole
sure the bad habits   low-potassium diet   fatty mental life
a list of should-haves   but I'm still thinking subtle   you're catching on, thanks

can there be limits   to the ways we can answer   these questions we ask
maybe, yes, and no   mostly we want one reply   we call her True Love
I love her deeply   but there's a kind of surprise   surrender to it
when the answer jars   or shocks or unhinges us   as coming at us
it's very strange/weird   /funny how we like a jolt   (before it's a brand)

All right okay yes

all right okay yes   totally affirmative   agree and approve
dumbing down hold back   not really remedial   a few precautions
not making progress   completely puzzled, confused   can't say how to cope
accept these limits   an institution's the best   come see us some time
now an old lady   in a coma fifty years   nothing going on

— Dear Sirs: Please defer   life. Yours truly, Unsteady.   Can I have a stamp?
Can anyone here   lend me an envelope and   a stamp? Thanks a lot. —
earlier, today,   I asked the girl at Hardee's   a hard one. I said,
yesterdayweate   hereandmysonlefthishat   diditgetturnedin?
what she must have heard   was, *will you marry me love?*   because what she did's
impolite, she *stared:*   behind her the fried chicken;   all around a buzz;
her new register,   the tray she'd prepped for my food,   and me like a troll

repeating myself   at different speeds until   turns out she had it
and wanted something   which maybe marriage would bring   if she wants it to
— Dear Sirs: I'm sorry   but your neglect of this case   will be unpleasant
for you and for me   until you resolve to help   Yours truly, a Friend —
then scattered applause   then shuffling feet, murmuring,   and we're out of there

The contest between

the contest between invention and harmony for your approval
it's a social thing creative versus normal we can go shoot hoops
or figure out how to make a basketball seem to float between us,
for example, for there are millions of projects for us to choose from
and in each of them, elements of agreement versus: surplus frogs!

representation's another slope of contest to be like, or not
which isn't so much harmonizing with beauty as with things out there
but like expression there's still a trust in language which needs harmony
in that we don't talk in single isolations: not that Vivaldi
worried about our esthetic problem or cared how we might answer
his proposition that linear melody works against the space
of chordal backdrop that the figure needs the ground actor's lines the play

we don't have to care about his problem either we can go mow grass
or start replacing the old cracked asphalt driveway and the tired sidewalk
which if it turns out will help our house harmonize with the Joneses' house
but wait till you see the interesting new stuff we're going to add in
light post base, curved walk, 4 colors of mixed slate from several quarries

Don't look behind you

don't look behind you   *it is all given away*   will I get it back?
relax, you're still here   stunning corpse of a mayfly   that's a spider's work
or not a mayfly   some enormous mosquito   yellow-emblemed wings
not bought at K-Mart   like the stapler set nearby   got in by the door
survived a train wreck   and survived persecution   but not the spider

I look back later   how could I have been so dumb   well it's chastening
bought lots of Kleenex   left piles behind in anger   no one will help me
went out for a walk   when I came back they were gone   all given away
I get to keep this   my bucket still comes up full   can't run out of it
fear and tears and grief   anger and weakness and wish,   envy, bitterness
I'd like to seal this   put stones in it and walk off   here I go walking
maybe I can learn   to give when I am needy   what else could I be

the pilots thanked us   smiled by the flight attendants   glad to have you sir
it might be lunch time   in the factory it is   the day's unstable
his homemade canoe   broke on its maiden voyage   not a rock, just broke
a breeze in its wings   satisfactions abounding   choose your point of view
or know your own role   glad you could fly with us sir   glad to be here sir

Instead of searching

instead of searching   identification of   what we've stumbled on
looks like mites to me   yes, by the headful, Harry   real teeming masses
feels like a bad dream ❏   I'm pretty good at spinning ❏   spinning allegro ❏
still *pro patria*   out on the country's roadways   long-haired good ol' boys
couldn't see living   *anywhere else*, that's his speech   which omits a lot

after the cold front   blah blah blah & kissed him hard   blah blah blah 3 kids
only spoke Farsi   "tongues" appeared, a mystery   signs of emptying
broke a spoke again   spoke about my spoke again   we will see what's what
we'll see your gumball   and raise you, ah, 2 whatnots   what a what is not
you could always try   too hard: can't be an osprey   can't be Mickey Mouse
can choke on your gum   but here's how you can get lost: think a thing is small
when it's not when it's   a landmark for example   or having a map

that's why all poets   provide orientation: readers might vanish
and why in this work   every fifth word makes up   a useful index
not quite a note field   but a gesture towards you   so that you can see
and so come to know   the powerful message here   otherwise perhaps
imperceptible ❏   if the index is no help ❏   I'm Bun; who are you? ❏

Shucks, you shouldn't have

shucks, you shouldn't have   God-monuments of Egypt   tracked by satellite
Junior Mints flew down   pissy-smelling homeless guy   made cool *weef* noises
rocked by the train's rock   Michael lives in Vienna   raw stuff for weaving
touch my blindness here   BurmaShave survived his youth   a lot of roses
left that Kentucky   "Quince" as a royal title   hot grease for french fries

row, fish, go swimming   tiniest amendment talk   splashed hundreds around
will do their taxes   the James Gang hideaway dirt   blowdarts with poison
not the Merrimack   will do their public duty   not the real McCoy
sang in small church choirs   QWERTY looks like a standard   amniotic *X*
I'm Floridian   went in and out the window   contained erosion
napped half (of) *the day*   (Issa, translated by Hass)   *no one punished me*
former junk bond king   Bob Hope, on the Bob Hope Show   folkloric research

I want to like you   I want (you) to like you (me)   come again, she said
that's why they're extinct   ridicules everything   cutaway model
some hills in Kansas   keeping hands off your privates   counsels the crazy
we're nearly kissing   had backyard drainage problems   lexical portraits
all at once the rain   and it was because we were   scored one hundred points

How the falls unfolds

how the falls unfolds: the top is two sweaty hours   through Eastern woodlands
you get there and wow   you can see far, and far down   a thrill near the lip
can you jump that far?   at Pipestone braves had to leap   onto pinnacles
twenty feet away   running, having practiced, no   *bodily* problem
but someone would crack   land just short, slip twenty feet   clawing and banging

fiddle-dee-dee-dee   music in the air tonight   poultry-farmer twank
great future ruins: the Madison Square Gardens   Vegas Palaces
penitentiaries   nuclear, waste treatment plants   incinerators
industrial parks   landfills, self-storage units   plain old parking lots
fiddle-dee-de-dum   who's late to the theater   who's getting tattoed
fiddle-de-dum-dum   who's so mad at his teacher   whose hands touch what first
who's in a war zone   greedy alliance's fault   old cold Lu-ci-fer

meet Eri Sano   she's come back to worry me   it's the grade she got
I like her truly   she flew to the States to see   the desert Southwest
she was 17   she didn't know much English   and her folks agreed
she's very stylish   even I noticed her shoes   metallic sneakers
on 3-inch platforms   thigh-length zippered vinyl boots   red pumps and high heels

Starting shivering

starting shivering   as the dream ended surf-drenched   climbing solid rock
narrowly missing   hard storm's squint-lidded anger   but I had no chance
to save the others   who'd gone farther out before   I'd even arrived
in another dream   I was a woman but now   I can't recall it
in another dream   I'd gotten e-mail access   and sent her love notes

yellow-bellied birds   in the grass and on the wires   zip-darting around
ponderous walking   *suhpwized a bunny wabbit*   with a clean white tail
intersecting lives   your path crossing my path here   one goes hopping off
the other keeps on   but that's a point of view trick   we would rise above:
rising beside us   just behind the new bank branch: sorry, that's not news
not news that stays news: but that's a pleasing target   if I've intruded,
my apologies   /I'm thinking about Greek food/   what's *news* is not news

ate pancakes Wednesdays   ate fish occasionally   often on Fridays
a normal breakfast: fish fillet, watermelon   posters of Lenin
calming sinecure   to escape guilt is a good   unless the guilt's meet
then to escape guilt's   irresponsibility: so quaintly stern; thus
return to nature   Snake Eats Fish He Caught Himself   you saw it here folks

Nice aporia

nice aporia   but it's true I don't know how   to begin, *begin*
a ceramic pot   class of objects which begin   as known things, clay lumps
paintings too just stuff   canvas et cetera plus   smeary goo and such
and so on achoo   I'm allergic to all this   much too clever too
I try re-reading   momma don't want no, no sir   picky eaters here

lowered what standards   you're like trying to escape   in jail with anger
all the horribles   no one knows why the mean dogs   and you out digging
shallow-humped tunnels   one called *obsequiousness*   and one *funny* one
diversionary   and *pumped up* and *untitled*   as if thinking it
means you got away   well maybe getting lighter   on your feet *will* work
see here how you say   the library may have one   a book on cement
or maybe downtown   in the old feed store you saw   they have manuals

humans like circles   I give to you, you to her   it comes back to me
so I can end up   roughly where I started from   improved by effort
by experience   and so you can learn from it   plus you've been amused
having your own sense   of spinning gaily around   no just a bit warm
heated by the dance   dancing through the horribles   overcoming that

SIX

Thinking who has AIDS

thinking who has AIDS   mere fraternizing these days   mereness of gender
with unsexual   fraternizing not harming   anyone can harm
anyone can drive   got my pick-up ready now   warmed up and ready
cooled by a heat pump   supercooled turbo "redneck"   spitting out gravel
swallowed then by sloth   the Amazon exhibit   thanks for reminders

say it isn't so   fighting the haiku legend   *A-bomb test victims*
no worse than Mad-Libs   *according to what I've read*   it could go forward
ruined men fenced in   such an experiment could   *like the Hitler camps*
but New Mexico   *no one is supposed to know*   my pretty kitty
anyway more than   a number of syllables   *warped flesh all over*
to cry about to   *some people just disappeared*   *witnesses who saw*
seasons of nature   a keen pang of emotion   quarreled about it

"palpable design"   easy to blame in others   yet without it there's
produced in Russia   maybe you grow fond of ice   a wild few it takes
had you thought we're through?   I've got some research results   o phenomena
held her silvery   in the tale till she turned salt   a moral moral
fought back viciously   we had really a slim chance   rival sentiments

You've got a hard-on

you've got a hard-on   don't be making fun of me   *it's you making fun*
don't you see, silly?   well maybe I'm starting to   seems slipperier
trying to keep up   more comfy back when oops now   about fly fishing
extremely English   horseracing, hunting, those boots   sensing a drifting
a push, a push-pull   god that's a banging somewhere   riveted me too

de rerum river   there was a certain pushing   her clothes just contained
and then spectrally   all the fish jumped out at once   we about shitted
then the toaster popped   distracted by poetry   I heard the fire trucks
but why it happened   that you knew it wasn't me   that later it was
you laughed at psych texts   well some people just do it   without fantasies
oh the hell with it   do you like those figurines?   if they're Dutch they're Delft
certain about it   can't remember reading it   yet maybe I have

really nice leg work   and when we got going there   your mom's on the phone
little ones in Paris   suppose they'd become famous   sinuousness is
disturbed their comfort   rented a Winnebago   saw the Lord's cactus
hoped to see the Lord   took a short cut near Denver   he wanted to fight
no room for his kind   you've got to see tonight's news   screw the camera

Frontage sumac wheel

frontage sumac wheel   dust enough unleashed barking   braking all over
made jambalaya   from people from all over   settled apartments
like the hand of God   door banging nonexistent   yard a mirage work
wound it so springy   scratched at the hub to get in   dust on books and hands
would have done better   stop being so sociable   strict thematics rub

to be, what is that   in any form, what is that   just leave the corn flakes
Kresge heiresses   Seagram heiresses Ford heirs   bunch of dead Wobblies
volume reissued   Enna, isn't that a king   sounds like *Gilgamesh*
old stereo box   used the merry looks of smoke   smells like planes dropping
stunned by the glass bird   and when the cursor just blinks   and fakes a dead still
sold the sand which ran   to the welcoming ocean   burned their trash again
do you remember   burning trash with me out back   back in Michigan

the frontage sumac   dust from the truck's wide tall wheels   barking dogs far off
sumac red by now   I'd have brought my computer   I'd have bought tickets
there's no one left there   victory bumping apart   spooling the purple
they creamed us so bad   if I don't come back don't write   swatted at them all
had to be bitter   a calm feeling of oneness   calmly sailed away

Feeling pitiful

feeling pitiful   asleep she kicked blankets off   and woke before dawn
the trunk lichen-flaked   even as a young tree old   unsure of others
it's getting to him   hat off in the fast food place   then leaves it behind
reading the labels   shoppers get nutrient facts   but no master plan
the tiny tree frogs   peeping their early spring signs   swelling the news wires

dialed, dialed on   half an hour of dial tone   guess the phone's broken
electric cherry   the look of the sun at dawn   breaking the hill line
breathes in, becoming   savors being-at-one-ness   exhales, returning
over his shoulder   into a squawk before him   defending her nest
a simple city   river, shops, market, houses   strangely deserted
elbowing forward   she saw all their spectacle   she had yearned for more
the very rock where   William, Dorothy, and John   said their last goodbye

freshmen, they made friends   eager beavers too early   to get their classes
these atlas pages   whole networks of roads diverge   lots of them in woods
you'd think, making love,   you could never fall asleep   but she kept me up
migrating swallows   winter-stiffened into heaps   warmed by sun they flew
that tarn fogged and cleared   fogged again and cleared again   again and again

Doing a study

doing a study   my lady, my lord, to see   if the world is round
we agree on this   those riches undoubtedly   an engaging risk
I just want to get   the hell out of what's boring   intending no slur
changing voices now   the mask crudely carved you know   you won't be deceived
I'm not getting out   but it is hard to explain   why I'm doing this

I'm not doing this   a divine afflatus is   a demon jabs me
I've lost self-control   no self left to be controlled   THERE'S NO ONE STEERING!
there was Mary no   it was Merry no Diane   there was Linnea
we knocked a wall down   following regulations   we built some new walls
corner cabinet   coffee table with full shelf   never yet a lamp
best times of my life   mowing the grass dog barking   lathe spinning smoothly
laughing in movies   sure, in a lot of movies   crying in a few

we drank a sheep's milk   strained & boiled it & drank it   we milked her ourselves
we planted flowers   geraniums from cuttings   we found wild capers
wild anemones   on a mountain path we saw   a carved stone spring box
the paths were marble   the island mostly marble   whitewash, salt, and dust
slippery pebbles   under the tamarisk trees   but a pretty beach

He sounds like a man

he sounds like a man   who's never been chased by dogs   maybe as a child
if you run or bike   in places where dogs run free   then you may be chased
the terrier-type   I met today/had no plans   really to bite me
just wanted to chase   I lost him around 20   tuckered him out good
adrenaline's great   my cadence was 96   I was yelling loud

let's go push the swing   there's enough story for now   time to digest it
forward-back, down-up   he was not named Lawyer-Fruit   a viceroy flier
he was named Repeat   he was named Algorithm   he was not singled
we had the whole list   she was on it too somewhere   she was Endangered
Easy was her name   like her father that Disgrace   the Trenches of France
Bonjour, je m'appel   a family of budgies   the modern methods
new tools, new schedule   walking by a man whose ax   whose water grindstone

she had the new briefs   the broad satin-strapped brassieres   she knew he could tell
please let them marry   so I won't hear any more   who has the paper
obituaries?   you want to read the obits?   I'll read the style news
I'll read the stock quotes   that guy, thought up Waterbaks?   he's profiled today
his company's hot   champion bikers love them   they do more sipping

Construction brigade

construction brigade   moving cannon one problem   moving pianos
his joke surprised me   making fun of eyeglasses: dad says to his boy,
beating off, *you'll go   blind*/the boy replies *I'll stop   when I need glasses*
six at our table   I'm the only one wears them   but he's harmless drunk
moving pianos   there is some science in it   ropes and cords not chords

your jury duty   quiet in corner knit knit   now to be more free
to be utter scree   once perpendicular now   lax or dejected
bent under his knee   hey that was a mourning dove   nice watercolors
here's an emphasis   those ideas made him sweat   the paper's curling
that's the way it was   he wanted what *she* did not   want to let go of
in a few seconds   a tornado's created   torn from the weather
marks of home sweet home   all over their small bodies   must stop watching news

vials of eel mints   such violent elements   valued cement mix
axiologists   is that what we need more of   or cars with huge sound?
I'm in envelopes   I'm on tenterhooks I'm green   I'm about to cross
the Jewish homeland   if Buddhists aren't pacifists   reading *Our Koran*
reported to do   precisely what's expected   then didn't do it

We've been here before

we've been here before   together here once before   together before
I'm sorry it's lost   those memories forgotten   lost and forgotten
the time we had then   talking being touched laughing   touching and laughing
wordlessly passed on   sincere but not remembered   split apart wordless
we were here before   lost to us broken apart   shattered to nothing

not nothing really   fractured/but reassembled   indelibly traced
but then resorted   constructed/but redesigned   mirrored/distorted
residual ghost   residually haunting   behind the mirror
old marks on the stones   as if inscriptions face-down   maybe I know you
maybe you know us   our great-grandfathers unknown   maybe whom you knew
a shape to our lives   we seem to have met before   there's something not right
no it's all all right   we've been calm here together   we've been calm before

now you have left me   without even my seeing   I know you have gone
I never knew you   speck in the eye delusion   I'm not sure myself
the storm was up there   in the mountains and not here   I hoped it was here
you were kind to me   seeming to be willing to   I never knew you
I hoped it was you   I hoped I might remember   no one's repeating

Such a sweet liqueur

such a sweet liqueur   definitely medieval   digging your heels in
let us each see how   what for us brinks are (sharp fear)   glass windows & birds
one day there's a clump   unrecognizable guts   — dog get a rabbit?
covered with green flies   a day later there's far less   now you can't see it
right there in the grass   all that stench and revulsion   broken apart now

one day the mountain   ignore your impressive list   can you? if so, climb
if not, check out why   I'm just saying what Frost said   (our details differ)
I've a new callus   on my pinkie's outside edge   (bad habits typing)
I still like to pose   still like having photos done   thanks Barbara
surrounded by them   little instruction icons   where to feed paper
how to use the soap   little hands pointing stuff out   signs if you want them
bought her a dummy   she's given it her figure   a weird thing to see

got to start a list   ignore those mountains again   it's a long long list
oh well fiddlesticks   too many friends to write to   let's buy a canoe
paddles shining bright   working on my J-stroke, man   don't like hitting rocks
don't like rocks hitting   to be stoned by your village   die of confusion
I mean contusions   recursion to violence   worse than the world is

Working part-time here

working part-time here   blubbering boiling over   trashed banana splits
outside aroma   outside room or offsite rum   words of an Irish
romantic auctions   happy to meet your gene pool   going out walking
signs of being scared   get a bearing beforehand   scraping the table
the table scraped *me*   what's so wrong with narrative   there was carrot cake

there was a huge bliss   bloopers were too abundant   even for part-time
a family joke   not that *that* means anything   wild trumpet vines there
offshore it still stank   *dumped guts of a natural*   *slaughter* a cycle
most interesting   on a day when all feels fake   yells NICE QUADRICEPS!
they loved prairie dogs   about time we went fiscal   pushed on through the seas
purely a villain   last week we wrote a novel   next time he tries that
sorry — my hand hurts   I can triple your profits   bored by bananas

if you're ever scared   keep your keys in your loose fist   let the keys stick out
between your fingers   then when he attacks you slash   right down on his face
it's like using knives   he'll fear he's been blinded, he'll   hold his face with hands
get the hell away   run screaming away so fast   and if you're lucky
he won't have shot you   that's what's wrong with narrative   evil and bloody

Apollonian

apollonian   viz., calm light clear cool restrained   selves dissolved in that
plateaued enjoyments   305 types of pear   of apples, thousands
steel tools clank nearby   softer technologies near   there'll be double prints
small wary saplings   seeking to be huge shade trees   trees of wistfulness
felt but not anxious   things acknowledged but not mourned   examined clearly

what loss we will feel   what huge losses we will feel   what we'll agree to
later let's check the maps   see where the stars have fallen   drive around gawking
got to get this out   trim back on that wistful tree   it's rubbing the line
power's getting out   dangerous environment   authority's worn
wearing the tight skirt   don't think it's an illusion   from our Virginville
catsqueak of a chair   Binky and Pinky are here   they're rubbing the rub
Sunday barbecue   Sunday see who'll play Scrabble   Sunday change the oil

she's intelligent   she's witty and she's friendly   and she makes good art
let's take stock in that   *Aktiensgesellschaft* something   he had a cobra
he had a new one   he had a problem so sad   who is this *Ling-Ling*?
dionysian   that's a proliferating   scuse me the earth quaked
tendrils, grapes, the wine   the full-bore sea-chantey shtick   hey I'm a model

This pivoting point

this pivoting point   fear and anger and ego   versus a calm love
hinging on what is   insect at my ear last night   seemed to want to say
might have been a moth   beautiful papillaries   who knows, flitterbugs
wrecked the enamel   left in the garden to rust   made it a planter
petunias boiling   out of an old kitchen pot   recycle, reuse

they blessed the buses   they'd have blessed carts and wagons   in the olden days
the national park   only one in New England   I exaggerate
that's not what I said   maybe, I said, east of the   the Mississippi
starred as a buffoon   shocked by what an insect thought   I've grown up since then
a different font   but making these assumptions   sucking these flowers
all these butterflies   pushing into each other   the big ones don't budge
except for the bees   I'm not worried what I learn   it has to cohere

you can't force it to   call it cosmic enclosure   galactic corral
we're here cohering   splitting by dialectics   stuff and ideas
momentary light   moment by moment changing   so these are the grays
you can call that white   these are powerful changes   "chagnes" I first wrote
root of our sea-chains   and James Cagney who starred in   & swans, their cygnets

Back to Piney Hills

back to Piney Hills   back *before the Romans came*   back *before this all*
now too much for us   he said his kin's all right here   no place he'd move to
I told him okay   but my family's spread out   Geoff's in Alaska
he said yep his wife   was from down Madison Heights   (just south of Monroe)
and he'd tried it out   but after a year he said   back to Piney Hills

rural is just shades   of suburban any more   4 by 4s standard
schoolbuses standard   satellite dishes standard   roads not as good but
not as much traffic   or inamongst the rural   suburban traces
we *need* elegies   this one laments, whispering,   the change of eras
people used to leave   the country/now country's gone   or going; wild's in,
inside, endangered   going frantic behind this   smooth sumo wall; still
firmly defiant   it's spotted an opening   —*something* changed subjects—

at first I'm refreshed   and then I droop being sad   never fully changed
never fully charged   but easily persuaded   —want to like the world—
and was restarted   like the old motor almost   flooded but caught, caught
and now can keep on   get all that nasty grass cut   keep working around
not making problems   but, finding them, find ways to   slip out and solve them

Earnest game of chance

earnest games of chance   reminded of humanness   that's cool we're not ants
they speak about ants   ants don't so wholly engrossed   in being live ants
in being ourselves   a little bluster and theft   a bit the noble
first it's to feel strange   then maybe strangely okay   maybe even right
but let's pry that loose   I'll rent a small jackhammer   they must make small ones

you know the Milky   Way is our home galaxy   which we look out through
back some centuries   they didn't know that at all   but they could see it
do we ever now   twice maybe in a good year   humans *glow* too much
you have to be camped   and the sky cooperate   well it's really nice
it's spectacular   it's a new product you can't   have tried out before
but you should, you should   and stop worrying, relax,   this newfangled stuff's
a phase of phases   larger than any phase and   we'll keep on changing

I'm happy to quit   I'm happy to be quiet   it wouldn't be kind
I've seen Greek weddings   Greek christenings Greek Easter   the blessing of boats
and that of buses   so why don't we go live there   see that's a real choice
you don't know what to   make of it/I realize   a bad example
I see this changing   I write letters home too/but   as we change, you smile

Dark and indirect

dark and indirect   a smush of light on the ground   just a little smush
moved from the clearing   beyond scenery even   awful conditions
opens ground to sky   I'm taking the fish to eat   but not this first one
threw his trophy down   no burned it on an altar   built it on the spot
built it, tore it down   redistributed the stones   a landscape with stones

out of the stream bed   from the clay cut and pebbles   with the slick algae
heaved the round stones out   reworking the complex crust   the thin hide of God
saying the first thing   saying the second and third   prolific children
colonies of speech   stones torn out to build us from   then torn back down flat
same as the trees do   lifting rocks in their rootballs   toppling and moving
the insect burrows   filling with moisture, freezing   heaving and raising
heaving and raising   you hear the spiritual   the highway rhythm

road work moving on   refiguring the contours   spiritual time
bodies clocking on   I'm thinking which kind of tree's   my true totem tree
he claimed *tree* and *true*   honoring their etymon   mean one thing really
I'm not so upright   something more earth-intricate   or so it appears
small clearings of light   say, a flashlight, a dirt road   the far dog watching

You & me we're sad

you & me we're sad   not knowing what's expected   *something* wonderful
but one way's to drag   stuff up/arrange it just right   I'd like your trust here
arrange it just right   as I was saying/so you   catching on, would feel
like the world had shrunk   gotten very tiny &   intense & with no
forewarning burst out   at you engrossing you &   then had new meaning

meaning its weight, its   full here-now-gone-then sadness,   shifted a bit &
seemed odd & new now   not a new meaning//meaning   newly felt again
yes I mean *again*   because we wouldn't do this   sad the way we've been
till we remembered   *here* may be a place to find   feeling again, &
meaning in that sense   when it's not really meaning   like clues & knowledge
discoveries &   intelligent stuff but just   maybe *worthiness*
a chance to shift &   let the load settle back down   & you feel rested

like you can pull through   can bear the load a little   more happily now,
that kind of meaning   is worth seeking & finding   & this is like that
but another way's   not to arrange it so much   to let it shift &
play out late at night   by itself if it wants to   and not to punish
it/when it comes in   clothes dirty, nose bleeding, &   awash in the world

Erased what was here

erased what was here   put something new over it   remodeled the rest
felt pure ambition   which is like feeling nothing   on the gray cement
look at these scuffmarks   these chair-dents in the wallboard   story a-go-go
very nice flowers   are they Afghani, darling?   (now you'll mind the queues)
soon the trains will stop   we've reconciled ourselves, yes   it won't all work out

how to pronounce *schism*   I use a dictionary   in my line of work
it's a legal tool   for income tax purposes   my sweet vanity
a thing which uplifts   what I don't know is whether   *brassiere* would fit here
it will probably   just sound stupid and corny   representing death
the stultifying   unnimbleness of habit   but maybe it won't
devoted to tests   testifying devotions   textual downdrafts
but the point's drifted   the cursor's all blinked out now   all its pathos dripped

go slap your own legs   your Arthur Murray routine   it's a time-two-three
time-2-3, 2-3   you know, Wordsworth, Coleridge   after the famous stuff
they just *talk* a lot   whinny, even, it sounds like   go ahead, boo, hiss
I'm glad I went there   saw Grasmere, climbed Helvellyn   helps the meaning out
helps it come to you   all the tour buses and shops   and not many birds

SEVEN

Dorothy's pancakes

Dorothy's pancakes   Ashbery's New York City   Andrew's obstinance
Cage's silences   Newman's *Stations of the Cross*   Tolstoy's Old Russia
Becky's gift, *The Gift*   Kathy's enchilada pie   Maia's painted room
Greg's model girlfriend   Madeline winning Scrabble   Alice Munro's stuff
Rigsbee's learnedness   Mark's ordered indirectness   Sybil's sestina

Dylan's huge dewlaps   Barbara's doctored photos   Craig's stick and mud work
Gwen's shrimp linguine   Ammons' geologic view   Chris's not stopping
Robert's rock and roll   Rosa's copper roses, throne   Bill's genialness
Wordsworth's self-knowing   Byron's exuberant angst   Rushdie's openness
Hardee's strange milkshake   Cindy's recommendations   Ed's huge paella
Ellie's cave paintings   Star's uttering profuseness   Gil's deep-troubled kids
Rick's mower riding   Jameson's *Postmodernism* thought   Heaney's Irishness

Susie's stage career   Robert's pineappled hamsteak   Allen's drinking on
Lucy's gossiping   Carol's loud frivolity   Jackie's acuteness
Brooke's paranoia   Mother's family matters   Ken's pleasing request
Hermine's mysteries   Katerina's German ways   Eric's caterers
Barbara's clay hair   Jane's Ophelia's stone dress   Karen's look at blue

Well what's been agreed

well what's been agreed   versus a chess computer   crystal ball express
a trisected arc   he never saw that service   conflated the spheres
smeared a little paint   oh what kind on what with how   there that's a baby
there that's a pattern   recategorizing it   still talking dream life
why would you use drugs   with wheat paste or hot glue gun   Raisin Bran's a box

had to hinge it here   the piano tuner cried   growing good legumes
easy to whirl it out   tempting to whirl it back in   better to agree
what's been agreed now   to loop it back's a forming   but an otherness
it's like a something   it's under an influence   it was after lunch
a rigor huffed off   sad about going for sense   well what's over here
(goes to poke with stick)   rags, ants, and a bent Coke can   but kind of pretty
pressed, picked, heated, dried: roadkill passing through its life   after its other

stage whispers offstage   I too wanted a program   you must let me know
he threatened to shoot   that car would have killed the dog   called the sheriff in
you mean the police   there's a law to enforce here   there's a low to moo
plenty of thistles   more kudzu than you can eat   roadside sentiments
Kasparov won last   the computer's closing in   panic enclosing

made rules, then broke them

made rules, then broke them   the damnedest thing you ever   can't follow it then
& picked things up from   graves ("Gone But Not Forgotten")   & etc.
like a *bricoleur*   that's from a book oh you knew   never yet laid bricks
superficial link   hypertext link maniac   that's what you expect
no signs here at all   of seasons or deep feelings   so much erosion

negative image   beside a positive one   sounded like Mahler
or maybe Bruckner   not this, what we talk about   but this could do that
this is more Satie   than Stravinsky, more Bartok   than say Albeniz
taking advantage   of "extended techniques"/is   properly the phrase
I saw a girl hop   by a 7-11   hoping for ice cream
this was a vision   she had lost everything   but enjoyed my smile
before I ride off   I want to do something nice   this was a daydream

positive image   beside a negative one   I'm the Lone Ranger
someone else talking   there's a buzzing around here   over-localize
let's go think simply   he would have loved to hug her   oh look: *butterfly*
oh look: *redaction*   oh look, look, look: a goldfinch   she extricates him
I'm finding it calm   I'm an All-American   a yellow goldfinch

This time tomorrow

this time tomorrow   where do you think you will be   in a car, a room
on a road, a floor   of a building with perhaps   many floors, rooms, doors
or lying on grass   playing with your retriever   looking for autumn
falling dogwood leaves   bees complaining for flowers   or by a window
awaiting cloudburst   light hardening, darkening   or fixing coffee

I've just won a prize   the E-Super-G Award   E stands for Ego
Super for Super   G for Gratification   it's almost enough
some of you may now   finally and at long last   feel belief in me
of course the money   will send my kids to college   which makes them happy
raccoon coats and such   rah rah siss boom bah Go Team   which is romantic
I mean they think so   which increases my stature   as a lucky dog
I'm the first winner   it's not like Nobel-stuffy   it's so very nice

I do have duties   I've only started to hear   I have to do stuff
remove shrubbery   take out tree stumps and plant new   remove old driveway
remove old sidewalk   have to rent a jackhammer   replace old lamppost
make forms pour concrete   trim slate and lay it in place   got to wear those gloves
but not tomorrow   you can put this hard stuff off   you know how you can

Maybe it begins

maybe it begins   wedging its way up slowly   like that no-leg guy
who scaled Half-Dome's cliff   many days winching himself   nights next to nothing
he had his own team   but he had to raise himself   that's the way it was
we were on the floor   one of those nights looking up   finding satellites
getting badly lost   I still can't believe we did   grown-ups, star-gazing

maybe that's enough   I found myself in a mill   it wasn't gorgeous
a working flour mill   and feed, they cracked corn for feed   all these old machines
powered by water   a metal overshot wheel   water coming by pipe
the dam it drains from   half a mile away they said   like a sewer pipe
if they don't need it   they close a gate and shunt it   into the stream there
and what the mill's like   hand-hewn beams and wooden chutes   with elevators
to move the grain up   to hoppers down to rollers   with little ridges

repeated and there's   bins of bran meant for hogfeed   there's weight-sensitive
at 25 pounds   sack loaders which cut the flow   when the flour bag's full
and there's the owner   old man whose sons don't want it   I guess that's the end
they sell new bushel-   baskets and feeder tubs and   hayforks and bush hooks
insecticides and   hummingbird feeders and prods   steel or electric

Kissing Emily

kissing Emily   hanging out with her sisters   kissing her sisters
could have been funny   or tender, or macabre   but it was tender
they talked in stanzas   four-liners, based on haiku   Emily did it
her sisters did it   can people be too wholesome?   these were fine people
not drinking buddies   but maybe that comes later   we were just kissing

all my dreams were mild   in one I became aware   I'd been there before
that's great isn't it   a little sinister too   you've needed something
you've been finding it   but till now you've kept it closed   or let it be vague
not to moralize   anyway I was anxious   thinking about Ann
if I'd been thinking   about Bill would I have been   bilious? or if
Hilary... but that's   obvious & I don't choose   that but to turn back
there are these caverns   pliant and decorated   kept for, kept from me

here's a deep folly   finding meaning in brushwork   oh it's there all right
a Corot maybe   stood on an Italian porch   held his own palette
stroked ochre bits *here,*   *here, here* and caught rocks and roof   in a net he left
catching us again   our nets seeking his sought nets   the landscape of dream
we're here, we've been here   another's gesture-record   pointing, pointing out

Something something dust

something something dust   mirrored the arrangement in   a magnificence
the whole lot of us   bounce legs stiff over field rocks   saying Lo and Ba
likely your time's up   pluperfect or whatever   had to refer to
in which an ostrich   I know you know what I think   tricky, now, echoes
it was a smooth wall   she offered her breasts to help   like pitchers you see

they should have lingered   & driven during the strike   like the other guys
no need to get there   so clean like after a rain   all catharsed they were
a day for napping   but they'd left nothing behind   took the book of dreams
squeezing two lemons   halved then squeezed them in his hand   broke a clay brazier
freely he gave her   not freely she his mother   his sister get the door
you saw that Pointer?   cleared out the Lonelyhearts gang   reach and take a tile
his chemistry set   his distillery glassware   robin's got a worm

caught it all on tape   fell asleep drooled on her shirt   on Easter Island
on a centipede   remarkable symmetry   cordoned off the walk
well it just seemed right   the freaks went outside to wash   a magnificence
fire makes the hot air   rode quiet over horses   over the islands
too happy alas   where the shore ran up the hill   shouting hey I'm home

As experiment

as experiment   oppositionality   free to roaming woods
your girl's good-looking   that's why he came on to her   why he dreamt downwards
covered with white spots   an eruption of good taste   not that the woods weren't
she's a new dessert   you almost understand this   you've been gathering
you hold a mushroom   gently you pry its heart out   you *never* say why

Thank You repeating   the mother who that thought of   the mother who milked
sure, capitalism   but there were those smooth smooth thighs   's'all politics right
terrors abounding   but some onlookers, always,   so far spared, do not
does Marxism work say   in India, India   of talking monkeys
it's cold or it's dry   in India, India   we take a look-see
the marks are erased   marks of erasure are not   made special for you
a string hanging out   it's okay as idea   fully spoken, SIR!

it were the doctors   we'd never come up with *that*   how they just probed in
what's this about *down*?   I've lost my damn (quote) (quote) keys   ivory waters
yes the Underworld   amusing little dessert   I sound suspicious
like I'm up to some   thing don't I that's the clue found   also there was a beach
some background music   a foreign tongued TV news/   /stripped down to phallic

Out of the pipe hole

out of the pipe hole   eight feet from the patio   someone's pet duck flopped
do you feel the chill   we will always be bewatched   so near to our heads
writ impartial books   thought like lexicographers   it was thought flopped out
then flew & left us   bleak maybe like limbs on oaks   wear your magic ears
don't call this defeat   built a duckhouse for the pond   not what I dreamed up

plot out a fever   versus making poultices   or shaping roof tiles
you dig you plant crops   you eat you wash up you sleep   you bury the dead
you launch some rockets   you rush through weird cosmic math   to wrap bouquets in
bouquets of cosmos   the over-and-overness   so unshoutable
just like here's a duck   it seemed always to belong   showed up and then left
in the first light snow: a woman organ grinder   a Weird, beautiful
sparrow-simulant   oh we're leaning on the world   full of rental cars

it's a happening   liberal sprays of Wite-Out   she slanted the ball
& watched it roll off   what appeared was Rolling Off   she has lost nothing
drop by tomorrow   same time & I'll show you how   best lay off the Zen
too much violence   you have lessons to repeat   leap out on the stage
the public dream-space   do your little business   hinting anything

Car door slammed on ear

car door slammed on ear   dropped & broke a milk bottle   got a Christmas train
oak parquet the floor   His redone breezeway office   watched Him use dumbbells
ate His piece of pie   picked up & shaken for it   crayoned the baseboards
a jigsawn worldmap   She at pine-swagged piano   Uncle Wiggily
rows of sewer pipes   picnics at park down the street   some game with the fence

help wash the new Ford   harvesting cherries for pie   who went on the roof
threw brick at some car   punished by sitting on stool   were They They were mad
side rails of the beds   (sharing a room with sister)   She wiped my bottom
pooped in pants must have   used a gentle warm washcloth   walked along to school
hid in tulips there   pretend-fishing at school fair   more stuff behind sheets
decals of bearcubs   the highchair near a window   must have thrown some peas
milk came in glass quarts   condensation-slippery   He'd always go off

Pritchetts were neighbors   the school's was my middle name   a scary movie
spiders swarming in   big as men & climbing roofs   a ditch two blocks off
up the ditch a ways,   a brick home for unwed moms   too scary to see
He brought Her cookies   fresh coconut macaroons   just two one for Each
follow-the-leader   playing whale with my sisters   whale under the bed

First he made a slit

first he made a slit   she started tearing at it   the thing fell apart —
of gender war just   another casualty — of   putting it that way —
no lives were at stake   NO fucking LIVES WERE AT STAKE   woke for a minute
did his Zorba dance   for a decent interval   a cooling-off time
now roses are back   the news got me by e-mail   we're all so happy

there's ocean; here's sand   of course the sand feels stupid   just lying, waiting
you don't have a case   no lawyer would take your side   unless you were rich
we rule that one out   you're just a dim grain of sand   that wave is so huge
it will beat you down   its arguments so utter   where do you get off
where do you come from   where do you think you come from   there's like no story
well yes and sort of   though mountainborn I remain   one tiniest part
weak but undefiled   broken, mashed, but untransformed   atomize who can

woods full of deer crap   look at you just screw around   a light snow begins
the fences fall down   certain tracks through here are theirs   my job: hold the bombs
I've got a live one!   no sirens for a while now   just an injection
welcome to Austin   the thing to do is sorghum   they did bring flashlights
saw a lot of skin   she got promoted too fast   they loved her to death

Pure quirks and few perks

pure quirks and few perks   each a burning filament   each its own fishbowl
he was some painter   added his own atelier   scripted sky slogans
pieties and prayers   painted talking rabbits too   on a wedding plate
no fish life so far   it keeps on drizzling like this,   there'll be sex crimes next
the trains in danger   whose loads are nuclear waste   derailing sure nuff

was stretched too thin there   just hammering on & on   deal of tensile strength
here's a meteor   crater dust kicking around   settling, infolding
by field's edge phone lines   not to say lonely but still   those voices' pulses
webbed all around us   over the long windiness   rung from the rank steppes
actual bus stops   a certain basic knowledge   I planted eyes then
the girls were watching   they wanted my autograph   I'm not hard to get
wrap your chain around   rev the tractor out it comes   stump with all its roots

guess we missed the bus   but we found a pair of hands   huge valley-sized hands
wherein our comfort   constant in-streaming of stuff   nest-weaving feeling
the bumps will smoothe down   impenetrably naive   the chic of ugly
I don't know you know   whatever you know you know   I know whatever
a knack of parting   a chestnut an acorn gift   opened the window

Shameless pilferage

shameless pilferage   got things placed on the right map   ritual brain dump
small bus stops: alarm   it's a bus without windows   on the sides that is
makes them yuk it up   a man invented Goofy   he looked just like him
he looked just like *him*   isn't that what I just said?   they can't look away
now Joyce in Trieste   buoyed on the hose of langwidge   rolling with daftness

I'm taking no steps   against it [winter] let it   snooze off its freedom
the first is the worst   they all buckled their helmets   flat to the floor crashed
punished by napping   then rearisen reborn   who's done this to you?
who'll do this for you?   the church has an advantage   shelter, and music
shelter *in* music   you can't fight the universe   by yourself alone
might as well stay warm   see what the group can manage   there now school's let out
let's check out the graves   watching them all is the gimp   weakness lubricates

her red carpet now   she's just spoken about it   her installation
from gallery door   diagonally across   the intersection
in cars and on bikes   people honked on it and whirled   40 meters long
ART MAKES YOU SPECIAL   art repays for regressing   ART IS OBJECTIVE
art is defiant   ART STICKS ITS TAIL IN THE AIR   ends as document

Four woodcuts today

four woodcuts today   five if we can count problems   it's either no good
or it's my best work   the others I claim okay   no bastards in those
it's like good manners   this one's a rude rude fucker   what's going downhill
a disappointment   they slam the door in his face   I guess I do too
the block hewed & whacked   the proof distressed, distressing   good just for kindling

part of me's now ash   oh there's a nice fire and all   part of me is ash
it's time for the blues   the mean the funky the blues   we're shivering now
pretty much for me   pretty much piles of manure   a dump in the woods
the torn sign thrown down   by a kid's broken bike frame   pretty much like that
like stuck in the mud   the fire's gone the sun's clanked home   I'm thinking; that's it
staring into space   wherever I stare's the same   moss and bird are space
that lousy woodcut   my pretending to be you   slapping at our walls

the I I am has   never once made a woodcut   you see what I mean
the I I am has   always felt the walls we're in   I blow up is what
I've never felt so   damn stupid all the time I   take this all to heart
sentimental fools   you and I and you and I   I'll give you a beer
we can laugh later   old folks weeping near the door   at least I found you

Gorgeous filigree

gorgeous filigree   down in the left-hand corner   obscured by a flag
obscured by a crow   a fig tree comes from the crow   it all comes and goes
on a wavy scrim   might pass for God can you see   it and then you don't
a country CD   massaging all the willing   floats back through to frame
a steepled vista   a leafless stand of birches   this must be winter

this is one vile storm   the birds couldn't have hidden   piles with broken wings
inland river fish   a river's tributary   that's us not bothered
a dog barks long, loud,   across the river, the fish,   and on the right side
a flashing red light   & the Sistine Chapel wall   emphasizing Hell
a very small print,   about wallet-size, glued in   twists if you approach
that is the whole thing   twists again diaphanous   might as well be God
fixed with bobby pins   bobby pins and chewing gum   whose aunt had a wrench

there is a still point   there's a point, still, to point to   & water, & pipes
I can feel your love   I'll be back after the dump   I'll go there, be back
there's a dead bike here   no teacup, just a handle   handle broken off
too frequent these tears   it's not poverty's problem   here's where the pulse is
that's the poverty   it's not the mud and wild stars   it's here there's pulse, here

Long parallel lines

long parallel lines   appearing, disappearing   the sun wrestling clouds
nylon sleeves rubbing   keys chiming as they dangle   these noises walking
made up for sweet dreams   did weeks of dirty dishes   ate the humble pie
got the weather news   derived it from the weather   dreamed about dreaming
dreamed about turtles   hopping backwards over logs   into the ocean

the mail van has come   not so tongue-pressed as Joyce was   not on time either
tell the old rooster   the one by the gray-green door   where the mud begins
looked in a puddle   the top ice had sunken down   still showed old tire tracks
rainwater on top   heard the whipwhipping of birds   saw them reflected
pleasures of clearings   open eyes of the dark woods   climbed a shooting seat
tall iron tripod   roughly corroded and braced   by bark-peeled tree trunks
love that new music   electronic collages   folks songs then Brahms say

dried sea spray on them   always cleaning his glasses   or barbecue smoke
had his own pen knife   used it to sharpen pencils   no unicycle
you thought I meant trains   train tracks to infinity   I just meant tree trunks
shadows on the grass   only when there's sun enough   I can't outsmart you
my god a real bus   real turtles playing leapfrog   really real really

Neolith heartburn

neolith heartburn   securely panting bunting   Dalmatian bargirl
all the wheretofore   whizzing nincompoop Fridays   ran out ran down gone
got the runaround   unimaginable cries   little seeds, for teeth
come on/the window   well you said yourself it's done   a monorail gift
growing like a bean   missed that springtime holiday   took a noisy nap

that's why they never   green ribbon around her neck   nerf balls won't hurt chicks
construction bonfire   principles of anarchy   canoed wicked chutes
dropped some extra weight   committed to a cloister   a menace to dirt
a *ménage à trois*   a man of true lightbulb racks   you think these are walls
took a junkie's chance   swung out & dropped to the sea   *coquina* fortress
electromagic   there's that great mushroom seaweed   more to the pointer
married a potter   for fear of being touched ooh   oo ee oo ah ah

General Haiku   warts all around his you-know   mud-dauber greetings
slugs don't hibernate   purple hippie bus awry   the whooping crane cough
German ostriches   menace to the Three Stooges   commitment errors
squared right up to him   painted through the tissue mask   glad to know voodoo
pingpong with cacti   heavenly succor began   polite applause wafts

EIGHT

Zero degree crap

zero degree crap   abandoned to cynicism   what the hell does that
meaner than Hinshaw   hammered Max into the wall   where the lockers were
or Jack what was he   or differently Tidball   smartest kid in school
playing with old cars   Sandy's dad loved classical   horny matchmaker
I could have married   Sandy's dad he'd have hurrahed   well what was her name

the idea is   finally ideas are   then there's the past tense
about it for them   drink beer & do the laundry   productive worknights
it's all the same chain   well that's going to be hard   drooling's all it was
I can't stand to look   she made him give her his book   copier madly
he called him putty   just as my last hit went out   thanks for your spaniels
really, thanks, I do   was those "screw-birds" they had here   like pteranodon
but they couldn't leave   at least not the fossil ones   time to clear yourself

look as we tumble   ooh that was fun but warn me   Jewish disc jockeys
billboards for bourbon   Birdwell a beautiful name   Katowski, Eileen
if you're here please blink   only one Blinky's allowed   flour & water paste
the patpat drum thrum   wasted away to mere eyes   he was throwing books
you couldn't have been   look at all the snowy peaks   more vitamins please

Sweet lord a mercy

sweet lord a mercy   swallowed so into a scheme   a scheme of new schemes
limpid I'm thinking   a mutineer's freewheeling   forget the pale truce
why should balloons be   bringing me down hurtfully   found a new fabric
like turtle eggshell   evasively synthetic   a darker palette
whistling were arrows   lone hoe in the acreage   any fool is we

any flood makes free   this amazing gypsum rock   thinking "Indians"
thinking "the Pope's nose"   a thought no a thought's a thread   sewn between namings
so un-thought of me   counter-intellect hup-hup   like throwing TP
across arenas   a victory-dance-thing like   emitting word-strings
you don't want to know   look there's a birdhouse how sweet   look a wee wren-like
kit AND caboodle   I'm just a halo effect   autopilot on
self-organizing   essays on expressionism   let's go swing a spell

the ditch gets deeper   wired hot with a screw implant   poor thing looks weary
into my alphas   the congestion festering   spotty stone circles
made my own driveway   once with big gray cobblestones   once with white pebbles
rounded by the sea   Apokofto beach-scavenge   ruin scenery
this might be your last   these could be your last read words   bye bye don't worry

It makes her dizzy

it makes her dizzy   going every which way   huge aviaries
pseudo rain forest   slimy stuff at the bottom   lianas, huge leaves
most things shy-hidden   who's this explorer nosing   look a grog's parrot
look a seldom shrike   steady pumpings air and mist   fish tanks down below
undeniables   got the window ❏ open ❏ sounds   mixed my digitals

there goes a letter   too late now you won't get it   or that date which fell
tucked in at sunset   safely in oasis ha   got-to-see green door
sand on this side and   sand on the other side and   pretty attractive
as if to say snow   suffice to say is no bung   missing a piston
hit hit hit miss hit   like that and some lakes filled in   easier walking
you can drain the swamp   volumes of obsessiveness   sneaking around it
you dig your channel   *to* the mess, don't start *in* it   nice cold air out there

you've lost your wise owl   vicious with regard to mice   that was too scary
becoming a mouse   what's that makes a tree trunk sweet   curvy, moss-shagged, rough
swam from Despondence   swam all the way to Question   found Desperate beach
marked on treasure map   hiked up Mt. Scratchchinalot   always foggy yes
took a hang glider   flew with cosmonauts toward Scorn   left for Tryrenew

From the weltered world

from the weltered world   in-line skates on the stone walk   people murmuring
train whistles car tires   here's what's going to happen: adjective-with-noun
and then noun-and-verb   and looking the same somehow   perhaps volcanoes
sprouting eruptions   eruptive sprouts beginning   shell-breaking changes
little rockets tweak   lots of sideways excitement   smudged by its shaking

who's the smug lanyard   pirouetting forest fire   here on the platform
please grace those blonde churls   into hominy ado   cities went under
most was backlit first   forget the internment camps   all under bridges
and under water   frying flies, boombox, steel trines   careened abounding
tectronic filers   embezzled dripsuit fogbound   oh what a load, Toad
rich witch can grill quick   watch your be-hind boy I say   I don't think I'm real
so why should you, eh?   no no turn completely round   the Plates have spoken

"Saw Some Great Programs":   unwelcome gravestone message   (but that sitcom *was*!)
welcomed her bunny   guess it's time to remodel   the moat is drier
earned by sgraffito   next time he comes around-o   small papier-mâchés
your window's open   you missed all the chanterelles-o   who stole my golf clubs
national insects   smashed their guts on the windshield   the car, air, wind did

Chimps with lumps of foil

chimps with lumps of foil   dropping & tossing around   stink of the zoo house
what a martini!   nice bouquets everywhere   solves a third problem
solves the shelter one   solves the food one well enough   bluff here about sex
lost in a beech glade   lost in a group of aspens   lost in the birches
lost in pines and oaks   nervous as a fairy tale   as a child in one

how should it end up   sadly the bridge we aimed for   we hit another
hit one another   it off with one another   got with another
to demonstrate it   each got on the other's nerves   the story pointed
pointed its/well look: it had a story to unload: SOMETHING HAPPENED yes
court ladies simpered   that's just what I'd be doing   if I weren't in charge
sorry it stinks pal   shouldn't be second-guessing   why, see, hardly, can
self-punctuating   tattooed plus-signs on his eyes   old Sluggo comics

so proud of output   of diversion of intake   a horse galloping
that could scare a kid   in or not in fairy tales   a thing to omit
no, to not omit   a little recollection   what's been left in woods
left in thorns in moss   in plain sight by the mushrooms   what's been left in words
little screaming puffs   year after year vanishing   desecrated graves

Try here for pity

try here for pity   (looked back to you this moment   to index sorrow
trained here to worry   (dragged his body down the street   flinching at the lights
thrown here in disgust   (hooked a smile around a threat   silly and ashamed
trashed here as extra   (drooped down like a cut flower   past the pickled dark
trussed here for abuse   (flogged marked sliced & so dismissed   orange-peel squash-skin

a word avarice   let's crunch that around to praise   to leave a tight spot
the sausage is gone   no matter where it came from   even the casing
the pipe truck's gone by   marking the road behind it   past the old smithy
I'm a Phoenician   that's it for explanation   from Monrovia
too many kids pout   that's not how you factor fudge   she did her slip up
aerobic grandeurs   *mes grandissimes* as you were   who's the expert Ace?
I had it a while   then the line snapped the line the   so I sat alone

let's review the case: you wanted something, but what;   you tried this for size;
you took your own off;   you put this one on to see;   somehow you lost yours;
you fear it's stolen;   you think you should blame someone;   you can't believe it;
you're certain it's gone;   someone is responsible;   this one doesn't work;
there's nothing like yours;   there's nothing like what is yours;   this cannot be yours

Your loving brother

your loving brother   there and back about 12K   wind worse than the hills
believe me you don't   little kids on these big bikes   wind in the gray sky
signs of patience, see?   so you can follow the path   decidings to change
not the revisions   stupid by someone's thoughtways   never-closed love-doors
those beautiful things   practiced autograph seekers   I'll not make you wait

challenged to do so   inscripted a poetics   followed botany
slips grafts cuttings soil   welcomed home the cooler air   had to be barked at
lonesome cat at night   hawk over me on the road   maybe a mouse here
that's what story is   motive, layers of conflict   and resolution
clarifying us   this has worth as therapy   as education
for the common good   if you're a hawk you learn "cat"   yikes if you're a mouse
or you could learn calm   identify with nature   whose great big mommy

why *does* the dog bark?   because the other dogs do   the plum had its pit
you need to be told   that's what the dog must believe   I won't yap at you
okay sometimes yes   is this resistance closure   to accept closure
what were we saying   sister you are my sister   brother I am yours
a final bit here   confetti more confetti   the parade goes on

A custom relic

a custom relic   to put pebbles on gravestones   here two on each one
not many graves though   only nine or ten stones left   and a tree what kind
a small high-walled plot   looked like a pomegranate   wiry & scrappy
no leaves out to help   but no pomegranate, no   not in this Meinsdorf
this Jewish graveyard   with the chipped-out lettering   who's remembering

speaking of graveyards: how about that Berlin one   still so akilter
back "when" ('66)   where I read *Paradise Lost*   the right book and time
no footnotes at all   sloppy way to read it yet   the *poem* stood out
whatever that means   given this stance against plot   (see previous poem)
not an easy pose   you put your left hand there your   wild right hand frantic
that's not too shabby   a Miltonic inversion   are they found in yours
some grassy paths are   garden snakes, other devils   cracking the Hebrew

whose house wouldn't fall   if the big house starts to break   that's a rationale
chip chip chip chip chip   compel the past to be mute   chip chip chip chip chip
lines of sacred verse   clunked off the gray stone like teeth   the odd fractures white
so the stones are marked   dumb chip mute chip dumb chip mute   had a stroke and died
birds carved at the top   fine scrolls and birds left intact   eternal pictures

On the other hand

on the other hand   let's check out Petrarch's notion   he loves a woman
who (won't) (can't) (doesn't)   or (zap) hence all those others   a powerful plot
for *some* of us hey   making a knot on a rope   as H. Kenner says
B. Fuller explained   can be passed down the rope (us)   looks like tradition
but what's just not clear   is one story another's?   ehh ❑ pull the plug here

think about the South   the Old South we used to see   Louisiana
Georgia Florida   plantation house chimney stacks   from the Civil War
in Alabama,   probably, washing machines   on the front porches
plugged in and working   just not installed up to Code   washboards still there too
wishbirds taking me   wishwards trilling at daybreak   repentant wastewords
what's interesting   when volume and mesh agree   the volume of words
the mesh of the form   something happens a bit odd   even that might work

my taproot's way down   my prospecting's rapidfire   the results oh well
whatchathink Tude-Boy   I'm wishing I was a sprite   not an attitude
I'll build a moat now   make myself comfortable   a banana split
data goose feathers   dative motorcycle gang   dayadhvam we know
"yeah yeah" (as punch line)   double pleasure kayaks whee   access verboten

Hard and gemlike flame

hard and gemlike flame   working against our moistness   this hazy morning
puzzles on the floor   a not-so-kind argument   gendered approaches
or how is it you   seek to solve just by image   not using the form
& me saying wait   find the four corner pieces   and the straight edges
but you say some blue   like that for the sky, some green   for the other trees

a set of twist ties   a set of horse-chestnut nuts   a lone paperclip
the thruway's so still   we drive with private access   ignore the strangers
can't let them all in   except as manipulants   others' analogues
soulmates and inmates   redundant equivalents   putty to play with
with nervous fingers   distracted speeding along   you're all too quiet
can we raise these stones   slip-slide around find a bar   give up try next door
dark interiors   dim lighting means less thinking   relief to go dark

that pigheadedness   it's a car crash for you yet   I'm getting off now
a little prize egg   tucked inside each boxcar load   I mean probably
you might not find one   in every single car   or you might miss it
looking right at it   and still never realize   maybe you'd eat it
of course that's a lot   many cereal boxes   breakfast mysteries

Made from tinkertoys

made from tinkertoys   for such a sweet appendage   forgot where we spoke
tightens the drama   whew already you feel it   arrow at her neck
her collar points down   big V accentuated   mob of ducks flew by
we say "heading south"   that big-time pay-out WHING WHING   as good for you, no?
overtopped, floated   many times on Ferris wheels   made from tinkertoys

made from tinkertoys   phonemic, tagmemic stuff   I wish/remember
you'll be there with me   stop slamming the door at me   digested it thrice
it took that service   some logs in the woods are stripped   crows notice me first
slim wintry pickings   long stalks of grass with seed heads   some dendritic shrub
(used vase provided)   also, hi, words and phrases   small games and winking
idea-meanings   along with ceremonies   sit here and now smile
a line of flashes   photographers' cameras   a line of them then

the big beech trunk's green   Nabokov writes it "Praise Log"   as the Lord, Dog, God
she's still a Druid   not the cannibal kind, though   would you kill a girl
I don't understand   I'd need to drink a lot first   or always from then
we had sweetness here   then the pirates intruded   now we've become them
only no courage   we heard a bent harmony   made from tinkertoys

Shelflike sporophores

shelflike sporophores   that, not a banana peel   more than just giftwrap
more than reused gifts   seem to tell you what you need   & you've played the fool
we're so concerted   something more than bad mushrooms   I could be more French
be more critique-bent   where you think he's got the goods   YOU'LL NOT FIND unless
were you told "Read this"?   not by a lung chute maybe   went a tad awry

try *bracket fungi*   it feels like I'm in a space   a huge arena
like I'm practicing   golf, like I want the big gold   only this isn't that
this arena talk   let's grab a beer first all right   it's a BIG struggle
mainly not to fight   got to go with the you-know   the walk goes out first
then it must return   practically though things change   no bombs dropped this time
an odd hill of hay   a normal flight of wood ducks   customs of marking
logs ready to truck   saw-mill marks on the stump ends   a locked cabin door

he said "al dente"   this *basidiomycete*   woods lore's worth much more
overpersuaded   I'm thinking "William" but no   it was "willing" due
mimes practice right there   we get some clowns too sometimes   mainly dramatics
little snatchy scenes   it's a big troupe as you can see   fill the whole place up
in no "time" at all   feel we've been here forever   stop it with those drugs

Dazzled by dancing

dazzled by dancing   encroached into forest mode   went nuts tormented
returned for more "oil"   constantly straying off-sprays   ospreys here loons there
lined up monks brooding   intriguing shapes of letters   *queynt* was a burden
monks with little bells   the privatized post office   we could say *tinted*
embrace her strong limbs   embrace her with good feeling   we're almost there now

born on an island   an island river island   (Thames estuary)
jumped ship for a ship   came to the New World & made   me, among others
why we have great-greats   so we can be descendants   nothing subtle there
sure it's subtle now   the process and been so then   but a difference:
you're a curator say   to make a retrospective   that's pretty simple
your painter's famous   already famous that is   you just pick and choose
to show new artists,   though, you should be poker-faced   Las bright lorn Vegas

straying constantly   a fling with chaos theory   later with fractals
only not straying   as no word means just one thing   eternally thus
let those kids scream loud   what kind of mothers are you   looking up their skirts
that's a precision   what *are* those flowers doing   that Georgia O'Keeffe
we toppled giants   through neglect but we had to   an island of bliss

What enters the gate

what enters the gate   a different strategy   a more polar one
a suburban grasp   the most frightening stuff's loose   roomy in the veil
they've gone completely   they get their lemons on-line   lookit it's a fox
we snagged crayfish there   we drove past a peach orchard   crusts to remember
all gross authentic   there's a drone flying around   parachutists' club

rousted out of weep   crimped like violets or wine   burnished with longing
where we got cornpone   when we first made polenta   why we let escape
bunch of weeds bevased   I think my gate is open   walked upon the stumps
earned a limper's right   bought all the cassettes he could   squeezed till it broke up
now an omelet   squeaky-clean compulsory   broke into a run
galloped from the house   left that hot farmland behind   found the wet cool hills
oh the pretty snow   so left a desire behind   a coddlestonepie

study the map book   Swiss cantons, eastern mountains   fledgling tornadoes
armed with their Bible   they settled here horse and plow   well it was here then
spatially remote   physically passed backward   driving and driven
Jerusalem thoughts   and at the butcher's always   kind conversation
in that line of work   you can be an honest friend   seeing what you know

Her terror pressed her

her terror pressed her   just for five hard minutes but   inconsolably
then a strange event   wrinkled into her deep loss: possibility
then she could be calmed   then the miles-high screams could fold   she could play again
yes, boundaries bent   but the birds have harkened now   such terror demands
and in the balloon   a thousand feet overhead   peace returns, shaking

and in the houses   lining her way home from school   curtains drop back down
courting couples turn   once again to each other   thinking what it means
each one knowing it   each knowing the no response   none really steady
our lights not steady   the lanterns we hold so high   not shining so far
just barely out to Hope   barely out to Another   hope of another
doing the same thing   terrified to cry because   everyone might
at least this way some,   parents, say, can help others   calm back down from that

some like to be rocks   they like getting to feel hard,   relied on, useful
others like the fear   accept fake rocks to run to   repeat it again
— whee we're being saved —   or because stiff, above that   I'm with our Lena
this three-year old girl   who went toe to toe today   spectacularly
inconsolably   for minutes she struggled with   well, no friend of mine

Not quite a radish

not quite a radish   no lousy understatement   not a smelly fish
a shining mooring   a greasy spoon for rich folks   a clump of angels
no wicked gossip   not quite a mistaken voice   not the quiet type
a true-to-form pal   a person who leaves early   a suit-and-tie guy
not the least concerned   not worth what you've spent on it   not de Maupassant

a reason to fake   a renowned French string quartet   a traveling show
not the Devil's work   not the keyboard he knew well   no well-bred slumlord
a little feisty   an unorthodox key change   a lot of filings
not worn and shabby   not the way to my quote heart   not the worst wurst are
a chilling rainbow   a tricky mechanical   an old contretemps
no wily rapist   no common garden grubworm   not a chance in hell
a few more touchdowns   a limited exposure   an orange binder

not yet a model   nothing but trouble so far   no princely fellow
a stately oak tree   a sadly missing person   a veronica
no land of the free   not an indifferent judge   not a two-seater
a regulation   an example of lava   a lure or a trap
neither die nor card   not even a chance to change   no hangover yet

Her body of work

her body of work   well first just her body then   the face to describe
a mirroring off   a central expansion in   a mirroring off
dark blond hints of red   not to stand right there and talk   her mascara then
inviting things in   excited for a while, then   moving on, moving
blond eyebrows even   afraid of not being seen   just a way to talk

a few grays also   a pressed tip of cartilage   adds a point to nose
uses abrupt signs   with fantastical wish-life   yields a to gain b
notable cheekbone   she loves her ear stroked and rubbed   plain earrings great hair
values being here   but *here*'s multifaceted   hot, mercurial
still a trim body   a little round and puffy   basically fit
treasuring such things   setting them in no context   even magic fits
large symmetric breasts   like the venus de milo   once true now droopy

so the work see-saws   it slides around slick and warm   a hard rush to end
not broad spreading hips   more girl-hips still and slim legs   and likes that tingled
and in this instance   divvies up its attention   there's a mood thing too
she'll get on top and   the mouth thing too tho prone's best   belly on pillow
hard horny time gaps   a complete switch in feeling   almost a cycle

NINE

Young guy who stutters

young guy who stutters   suddenly I see the twigs   bears a patient child
what did Stevens mean   the sky *I* see *is* true blue   some branches are white
please spare some slop please   most are gray many have green   did free acrostics
dismissed as bourgeois   not a nice way to kill them   used a creosote
garnered confusions   tried to feel a Ganymede   freaking crummy plague

they all talk trashy   you must have heard the gate squeak   irruptive silence
articles of fifth   a collusion of measures   you crashed through my sleep
overfond of walls   toothy can't forbid himself   a red date feeling
reddened with feeling   what are they getting to there   who's that getting laid
they're talking in halls   hey but I'm not sinking down   she hassled him next
they then her hassled   wrestled or we said *rassled*   slim moonlight monsieur
slim as a coon's ass   a starving little street rat   I'M FEELING THE SOUND

our confession's plain   mystically preprinted   anyone can see
horrible coding   looks like a dictionary   one plot is older
the skeleton key   when I stumble a bramble   to dig winter graves
used a jackhammer   they loved and they got older   Eden going bald
you can just eat snake   find no tact in a monkey   do we like lamb's tongues

From a hunter's perch

from a hunter's perch   ask the etymologist   clear the barm off beer
grids of roads and woods   so much is rot's byproduct   woolly mammoth steak
slickered his hair back   a deer walks there should be shot   you must come at dark
into early light   *fermenta* are Latin yeasts   don't deprecate one
to praise the other   they'll probably cross in range   you must stay awake

who often alleged   weird-word-battery-powered   foreign customers
advised the princess   among the shabby changelings   loved *in extremis*
not willing to play now   conditioned circumstances   an accounting one
I'm a bouncy boy   if diamonds are my best friends   we visit the stars
disgraced by, postured,   an African birthing chair   hog-nosed or rat-nosed
feeling pointed at   not knowing the gun's power   a screw turning in
turning some secret   tighter into nothingness   blasted and kind of

I don't want to know   probably a recording   constantly on fire
window blew shut, shut   possible to smoke up here   use the small jar though
two leaf-moths flying   just leaves but the right size/shape   will you drag it home?
I'm sorry as if   banged her mop around so so   once might be enough
the bus is still there   go get on if you feel like   ya sas, ya sas back

An open casement

an open casement   thinking about a bike trip   ambered red dragon
church, graveyard, some cars   maybe tackle the U.S.   peeks at her collar
kids pass on parade   that means going west-to-east   her boyfriend did it
horse chestnut and oaks   our prevailing westerlies   a professional
sounds of hammer knocks   start in L.A. then desert   he's into kinky

the post truck stops there   three days of pure misery   X-rated film guides
window can blow shut   if you're going pretty hard   she tries Dream Dresser
none home at birdhouse   more if you're not so you must   the latex outfits
a bluish sparrow   then to Flagstaff where it's cool   iron and leather
tourists come weekends   plateaus buttes and dry mountains   she won't check out whips
construction saws buzz   then the baking plains and wind   he'll take care of that
a UPS truck   the Mississippi valley   also they have oils

a little white truck   midsummer humidity   each day a button
two church bells sheltered   the washboard Appalachians   her shirts open more
little iron rails   then it's coast down to D.C.   till they're tucked in free
red tile roofs and stone   that would be quite a summer   then the term's over
fast-moving clouds now   or there's England south to north   Beautiful Girl's gone

I've got a booklet

I've got a booklet   yes it's a bit depressing   have you got one too
partitions of air —   too cold for the ostriches —   briars stretched in woods —
contents not listed   that is the real contents aren't   yes it's very long
yes it's very sad   a sad nuthouse collection   I can't hear you now
why are you shouting   nakedness grows budvases?   you're not coming home

I pull in for gas   everyone's just been killed   Mailer's in what health
fumes everywhere   I drive off then it all stops   *then* it explodes wow
which signs will you use   when you want to get beyond   *Postmodernismus*?
I'm racking my uh   something the corner pocket   they voted but gee
see them there inside   them big bosses like us here   I come from pine cones
pine cones & nerve gas   I've been up in the tower   held the cold door knob
sighted down the street   I'm a smiling whirligig   well hell so are you

pulled his door open   I was Mr. Savageman   That's my girl there bud
all the guys hurt hands   dealing with the firecrackers   not me I held back
you always seem to   okay here's a problem: Date   blackface minstrel shows
they climbed gracefully   an old European pair   slim, wealthily tanned
but old and climbing   they knew how to pace themselves   and almost beat us

Another way in

another way in: you're being asked to join us   you're expected; yes
you don't have to come   you may even have reasons   for getting out now
if it seems too old   the host sadly known to you   winding the one horn
maybe he's too rough   no need to spend time with him   & his friends, what friends!
just netters of thyme   since the heave-ho's been given   change the scenery!

we're in a canoe   kingfishers dart down the bank   loons croon right at us
lots of small rapids   the current's got its own bed   what the hell we miss
we run hard aground   okay we have to redo   then it's set up tents
over and over   there were moose, reports of bear   a day of cold rain
that's the Allagash: or once earlier in Maine   in Baxter State Park
the Wassataquoik: set up camp in a lean-to   went skinny-dipping
the whole family   Maia was 12 Andrew 9   they both got across

danced on the beach there   we were so proud-primitive   so cold and mid-stream
she all waving limbs   he imitating her moves   she with pubic hair
barely budding breasts   he a satyric Cupid   all full refreshed
& yet you want more   treasure map, flaking blueprints   well the moral, friends
— don't *play games* with me —   — don't *throw tomatoes* at me —   anew, and exit

Insistent ambling

insistent ambling   satiety undreamed of   redundant pressures
stupid as a tree   hanging in a cliffside niche   that's inspiration
a farmer's patience   the seed's radical magic   taking what's given
with glee resigning   lonesomeness lakeland lagoons   glass shines in gutters
shoot bottle rockets   an encyclopedia   precise dewormings

a surgical heart   pass these vipers gently on   or remarks, or shards,
shares of good fortune   must be enumerated   walks in a slow rain
insistent ambling   beneath notice so not done   got the cart-jiggles
forged allegories   cat-speaking about forges   private not just strange
brushed it the wrong way   not the same as repeating   insistent returns
squelched a false detour   by attentive editing   got on the phone hurt
my play-companion   let me show you what I've done   it will be more fun

I can't play with you   you must play my way with me   weren't we bored before
look under the beds   things scrawled by the dust bunnies   rain writes in the dust
an ultimate text   then washes into itself   a whole insistence
I walk as near glass   silly bits about maidens   went collecting tales
they had their effect   reconciliation with   so unsayables

"Ostriches," he thought

"ostriches," he thought,   "I'll make raising them my last,   my true business"
deep *in extremis*   a spectral organ music   filling the bedroom
the mournful footsteps   friends going back and forth as   if checking for mail
light was breaking up   into harmony islands   packs of jostling tones
and the music too   colors filter-shifted warm   (like *South Pacific*)

many were quite bored   they took their white sneakers off   they smelled their own stink
it's possible then   to sit in an empty church   discard all soul song
or to be worn down   to a new degradation   to give mourning up
it's possible then   to trifle, to slurp soup, say,   sentimentally
there were soldiers there   better men than you were, Jack   not frightened by ghosts
not seeing ghosts there   not making ghouls from tree forms   always on the go
and whose way was it   always to be molding mush   or panning for gold

he twists the sealed tube   has a certain private dream   then another forms
his common discourse   slips us back to violence   we gawk like tourists
they upgrade Hubble   it comes by television   against their stale rage
lava lamps won't do   and kaleidoscopes won't do   the various birds
plants, animals, genes,   secret astral insights, what,   my true friend, will do?

Once upon a time

once upon a time   there was a good perfect boy   he knew what to do
and just where to go   and his friends were illegals   (could have been *legion*)
who'd waded and swum   stowed away or just drifted   or flown small planes in
some of them worked hard   others drank or at least fought   but he was normal
and also legal   which explains his followers   his stylization

his beautiful cars   the women of all races   the strange sounds and smells
so it has been told   [*Hey, that play was* Purple Dust*!*   *the one I mentioned*
<might your workers quit?   or say, "withhold their support"?   all "get sick" at once?
if they pull the plug   your English castle falls — to   be rebuilt again
for the play's the thing>]   a step-step shift to drama   starting from a tale
wherein the hero   turns out to be familiar   a weak sort of guy
who gets off on books   likes violent videos   hangs out with dumb friends

but has deft balance   a resonance you admire   until he cheats off
taking his mirror,   where you kept seeing yourself,   without meeting you
your luck's improved though   it's not clear exactly how   but you keep smiling
feeling your value   indeed feeling your valor   you think you're scrumptious
and then self-conscious   so much feeling and beauty   he sneaks off to brood

Flows in from the woods

flows in from the woods   from the chalkdust of blackboards   the engine's idle
a pile of carrots   left for the deer but rotted   from the tiny news
— gravediggers must use   jackhammers on frozen ground —   — a Blackfoot dancer
who helps children see —   flows in from novels from birds   from borrowing keys
from duck and rooster   from a cold church's organ   flows from the seawind

and flows out again   memorial and optic   offer of a hand
withdrawn into dance   and so expanding desire   flowing in from trees
from seaplants in tides   flowing out without rancor   and flows in as light
and flows out as breath   flows in as the meadowlark   flows always with steel
from knives used in war   unthinkable bomb rockets   from minnows in streams
and out as caress   as pulling you toward bed   flows in from your eyes
and out as caress   as adornment and as grace   flows from your great fire

from Mexican roads   from memories of dumptrucks   from bags and boxes
flows out as airmail   as pattern as Persian rug   flows in from others
flows out to others   through mysterious filters   through an eager pump
flows in as birthdays   flows away congratulant   in as a weak lamp
out as a tower   in as smell hair your moistness   out as jubilee

To make an altar

to make an altar there are many ways to start a thing you cherish
relic or idol or even an idea viz., “holy” or “God”
you could reverse it construct, say, a black altar to celebrate doubt
instead of goodness death and disintegration not lovingkindness
or you could just start it’s your job, here are the plans calls for nice walnut

or as janitor a black man working alone look at white folks’ mess
the same kind of mess night after night after night gets to you a bit
you save the old foil you start wrapping stuff with it light bulbs and boxes
you start storing them in the old alley garage they start talking up
you’re shocked but listen it’s not the God you’ve wanted this one’s more stringent
you’re going to change you’ll have to make adjustments it’ll be okay
you can save this junk you can save the stupid world wrapping it in foil

so that’s an altar a prayer space, kind of arty a dim, dirty glow
or you might dream one then go out across the earth you and your children
your children’s children and so on seeking a thing till it’s all just seek
life shaped to a quest hunting for a dream altar you’ve got to stay strong
you run marathons you send roses, write poems you’ve a certain look

Hot tingling panic

hot tingling panic   not the way I'd thought to start   but got home the same
exploring my lot   without fear though it's all one   (you get home the same)
winds will blow ha ha   they're still not learning my stunts   of course I've moved on
well past the black cats   caviar and neat red cars   they're still wondering
back to the at-hand   were we both wandering then   perhaps we just met

we're near-desperate   we want to be drawn away   we want "nourishment"
(open-mouthed feeding)   to be obliterated   just logs in a pile
not that you've asked me   what my opinion might be   but we also want
no part of let go   no part of gripping suspense   no part of tall tales
no part of postcards   their clever little puzzles   there's a blur right there
below the lightbulb   a hazy point of white beard   a man with laptop
a nasty night out   but you persevere you must   home's not on the bus

I admire you here   struggling through the stringy words   in and out like me
I'm surprised this works   in its way I know it does   — a love note, with kiss —
now back to the hot   spot not where fat pots trot out   back to ornery
I can't keep it down   no point in telling me to   there's another wall
I'm bouncing against   genetic Potato Head   mix and match and mix

Lop the egg top off

lop the egg top off   grind the salt grind the pepper   bread with marmalade
no, nasty plum jam   tuckered out from seeing films   a bit of a head
not films, prospecti   not prospecti, reportage   still tiresome, drank beer
dust falls to the ground   filial tobaccostore   I just fixed a need
syllabic detente   rip off some pizzicato   open your (eyes) (eyes)

who would pay to see   a fifty-one ring circus   even with talent!
and we've got talent,   two hundred eighty nine stars   and most speak English
but you won't know that   swept away by violins   tingling the big stick
she was, for her ends   is it love or sex that's weird   we're going backwards
soon we'll be farming   believing in politics   no really we *do*
it's just a vestment   no, it's just an investment   no, it's a remnant
it's a little crumb   not even worth invective   whose truth do you want

there's too too much noise   a nice pint's hidden in there   darts now, then the show
a line of sparrows   they wouldn't stop that bouncing   then she banged the door
I'm slow to anger   that's something ridiculous   not owning pencils
well we had to grub   a sort of wine jello thing   a rough surrender
the rapes that went on   one could write a book or two   and the crude bathrooms

The window blows shut

the window blows shut   you wake too soon sweating nnhh   clamps on your voice box
on your aorta   no no get up go pee wait   not on the seat lid
open the window   think black clouds tearing around   cotton candy whirl
licorice flavor   you'll have to clean the machine   get it back to pink
abrade the scratches   its refined graffiti   gears up with the wind

it was just a truck   papers being delivered   a line of errands
look, ads for faxes   that was a bird, or a leaf   splashed its homelessness
a nightmare nightscape   whanged his hammer to make sparks   felt the fear of God
clamps on your voice box   recycling like a comic   do the good stuff twice
feet planted firmly   stuck in the mud as it were   scarecrow clothes flying
always a current   always a canoe and need   to flow and control
not to go free-fall   through the bruisings what the hell   try maximum speed

sucked up to boulders   couldn't take the rejection   *why won't he love me?*
just keeps forgetting   doing everything odd   not how he was taught
that one was a bird   who can tell under these lights   scared of standing out
that limb broke and fell   left in a huff for the West   started a new clan
much later rejoined   a Coke bottle in the grass   not much road kill though

Light blows at the wall

light blows at the wall   the curtain heats and swaggers   I'm in a bubble
the funnies were here   now it's all agriculture   bummer to hear it
we should be flying   take the short course in magic   now we are flying
there are lots of birds   more than you think, just walking   some are really mean
duck, run for cover   counting to five, then nine thrice   let's walk to the pond

let's see how this helps   displace the meaning question   with the mirror mode
sounds pretty simple   now you try it: don't worry   what it all might say
if it could just talk   and throw high for all to see   new sprig-signs of spring
disco mirror balls   reflecting faceted toys   which bounce among friends
which friends throw again   in order to be bouncing   throwing and catching
you should snag one out   slip it into your pocket   study it later
the polish should help   you can go on to eat it   should be edible

I have missed something   go to the bathroom a sec   come back to puzzles
a new set of books   someone else's pens and pads   dust on the laptop
you're Rip Van Winkle   or there's been too much building   or you've lost your list
coded in your watch   the e-mail walkie-talkie   Flash Gordon would have
fax buttons flashing   seasonable melodies   bound to the network

And so, on, on, on

and so, on, on, on   we've a sentry kind of job   the guard must be changed
the news inspected   intrusions closely perused   as trees find a nail
swell to surround it   committed to the next best   want to be normal
can almost see us   classic beeline ensemble   a divergence done
indulgence displayed   a fine old apiarist   bumps look like a rump

why's the water fast   faster by this cliff than there   there by the willow
he went for a walk   he met a forest person   one never returned
in the rocks a tale   from the sandy shore they swam   pushed the body boat
flames finding their way   the body or boat will burn   both ways sea gets both
the swimmers get back   dry off at the fire, drinking   so much for the film
whatchawanna do   go out for some pizza say   or that great chicken
test out the height stripes   at the 7-11   that's a sick detail

start to hunt for spring   thinking about English birds   Greek and German birds
flowers, cris-de-coeur   Gruss Gott and follow you in   time for some Trident
Caesarean birth   *gave into* is more like it   "rainbow" is too short
birth to rainbows   daydreamed their flights of arrows   3 strikes and KABOOM
this CPU once   messed around with processors   got its diskette jammed

Rolled up art posters

rolled up art posters   had to be left in the car   too costly to mail
four, five weeks later   near Paterson New Jersey   were no longer there
but the car made it   covered with thick engine grime   took weeks to get clean
this is how it was: in Lübeck, drove by Mann's house   found the ship's agent
left the car with him   whose advice was *take* the tube   (too big and awkward)

there was Picasso   from Dresden Cellini from   Vienna Dürer
from Nürnberg Rubens   from Berlin crackpot Rousseau   from Hamburg Cranach
from Stuttgart maybe   and Friedrich, Mondrian, Klee   Kirchner and Nolde
from who knows or cares   list a bunch of German towns   I'd gone to them all
bought cheese in Limburg   the whole schmier but overspent   hitchhiked to the sea
to Travemünde   for the Copenhagen boat   nursed a beer till two
in a little bar   The Mamas and the Papas   slept on a park bench

near a Ferris wheel   there's an amusement park there   reached Copenhagen
had a room one night   but the second, park-benched it   close to the Mermaid
then waited for Tom   a good angel to me then   who came in by train
still no bed money   but at least we could both eat   both slept on benches
though some cop came by   at last made our flight but who   knows how we got home

Why Pooh's not afraid

why Pooh's not afraid: Robin will take care of him   Robin's always nice
and about honey: he gets it when he wants it   the big picture's good
he might get too much   need to sleep it off a bit   maybe it runs him
but most of the time   he's an adorable brute   a sweet kind of guy
with nothing to fear   who's going to bother bears?   and he's lots of friends

old-fashioned, but not   a bad mate if you're Ms. Bear   looking for a home
just don't talk dirty   Pooh's just like Tom Hanks in *Big*   you've seen that movie
where Hanks is a kid   in a grown-up's body (Pooh   always looks smallish
so it's a failure,   that comparison [not *Big*   — maybe it's one, too —
but this isn't Film   Reviewing 101 and   *Big* isn't our job])
Pooh's pretty sturdy   and would perform pretty well   his duties I mean
predictably dull   but the missionary's good   at least as a base

Ann Landers on Pooh   would say about what I've said   with extra advice:
he's a bachelor,   so you'll have to retrain him   as wives always do
but if you want him,   Ms. Bear, you must go get him   try a rare honey
say cactus blossom   from Arizona, cowslip   from Essex, or wild
Delphic thyme from Greece   be punctual, and honest   or he'll mix up bad

TEN

Found the woodpecker

found the woodpecker   harangued the hell out of him   spit woodiness out
dove through owl pellets   used a mother tongue loosely   ah a shrew's poor skull
none knew him so well   none better than this hard owl   who shrove him so clean
not my vinegar   would have done so good a job   need one to lose one
so poor they had to   cook in potholes yuk yuk yuk   made sandals from tires

double-jointed hips   (hers) just wasted on stud me   what easy entries
or that red Corvette   (her dad's) with mammoth engine   bewildering torque
not Lewis not Clark   not LaSalle or Columbus   who seemed so simple
we were all thinking   I'll be Magellan but live   I'll bring back the gold
but in the real sheets   or the curved canyon highway   can't think what to do
please adjust my knobs   the mood swing button's been touched   enter alias
next to Any key   their favorite song, Cheri   a pause for hygiene

our theme of free love   so long as you wear a glove   Condomania
a popular store   supporting these rituals   are they advancing
best go see who's there   no one, he said, and fell, speared   we found his notions
stacked up in closets   behind the old washbasins   filed after Egypt
in the Death Valleys   *National Geographic*   sold us as birthright

It’s at cerebral

it’s at cerebral   downshimmering lips who touch   having stepped right up
so heavily cast   if it weren’t for ego love   I dreamed of Woody
Mr. Allen who   triple X-rated showed me   he called it “clit show”
a Chinese woman   lay there her legs open you   sat and studied her
as without moving   she enlarged and moistened and   opened herself wow

horrible to have   these things to live with to have   a little snow fell
that was kind suet   is it that someone has raked   no one dusted me
the way they treat me   old dirty man in dust traum   they’ve got their firewood
they threw it in here   some has banged my back my head   my eyes are weeping
banged my head down there   stepping out of the tourboat   the sealevel caves
a fringe-stalactite   they were smaller people then   it’s a magic world
headaches are timely   look how they bring the letters   after one two comes

sure sure let it go   they have to turn around there   they hit all the doors
speaking of marked doors   you’ve seen the bronze ones I guess   those years of sootstains
I’ve been left swinging   that’s another kind of door   checked and doublechecked
yes we’re roughly bright   lightning-brief and shocked to be   from oblivion
into history   bound to be switched at the end   have you heard the news

Old country living

old country living   *every house has its dog*   who used to say that
who tears the turf up   out there between the pine trees   it's all nostalgia
snow showers then sun   staying within the moment   I've not forgotten
a series of peaks   they call it *running the fells*   that's an extreme sport
we'll all *crash and burn*   but there's almost hovering   helicopterwise

now the helices   she said I've got to kill you   but she na gonna
cause I have the tape   and I'm not putting it in   who lives underneath
a bush so greedy   not to accept a whimper   no cry my baby
papa will try hard   buy you a new VCR   a new *Superman*
you can't imagine   how much I wish to please you   my meager stories
icy ironies   continual transfusions   slipping and then not
that tear in my eye   something's wrong that's why it's there   you made some response

completed that point   moved on to this next title   made a crummy film
met at the market   swept in by his momentum   no no there he goes
his parade returns   emptyhanded time for wine   why here's a fresh vat
one day they will care   they'll collect your peppermills   ants carry splinters
that's how we get them   red foxes carry rabies   don't smoke right there then

He picked up the book

he picked up the book   a Disney book about fish   lots of nice pictures
he's a fisherman   *Mediterranean Fish*   maybe its title
looked at it awhile   turned the pages, studied it   ten minutes or more
but the problem was   his hands had it upside down   he couldn't read it
but even the fish   (yes, latitudinally   *near* symmetrical)

what we want from books   would be first how to hold them   then how to read them
as you need to know   first how to hold a hammer   then how to pound nails
respect for your tools   in order to use them right   and then get fancy
first, legs on a lathe   then 18th century work   intricate spirals
lacy bric-a-brac   stuff you can't do the old way   nor just on weekends
not to shy from it   but to know the potential   to be connected
it so beautiful   so strangely put together   from what's here on Earth

it's good to be here   with all you beautiful folks   we should all feel that
it's strange and lovely   we can't do everything   own everything
know everything   but it's all strange and lovely   a tire iron clanks
a truck rumbles by   there's that kind of work to do   freely also this
toymaking for fun   argument used to persuade   words *do tell* can that

Shuffled past the pool

shuffled past the pool   extremely short manikins   volcanic photo
constantly hissing   which wasn't the word parting   he swore a tureen
the egg bent backwards   behind each huge door a dog   some ferns are friendly
gave up here did he   dreamed of give them what they want   inside the squirrel
this time we had stars   brunch came with a patio   snowy spring flowers

please tell a story   please use one/similar voice   whipped around and flipped
M U it began   memories of Hawaii   alien-phobic
how do you start this   please don't be deciphering   think of Diamond Head
who would you vote for   multiplied with tiger sharks   bungee-jumping's steep
one body-pierced nut   she said I've something for you   threw dessert away
misplayed the damn ball   struggled into the square root   look what we got here
waited for their coats   had to get the floors redone   went to Vienna

almost died a lot   thought she'd heat up lunch with it   an ugly broomstick
an island formed it   clipped his badge to her waistpack   quenched the red hot rod
new printer driver   smiled for the broken hearted   excluding laughter
free to get a beer   silhouette obscured the sun   let's test your semen
velure kind of feel   chopped and dug all afternoon   miserable wonk

In vino veri-

in vino veri-   *tas* fire-frenzied darkened years   which came by pretext
which slid through the gate   hunting bones in rubble *in*   *vino veritas*
in vino veri-   *tas* back to destroyed moment   revenge and fear-hate
or from a small stroll   accidental contact *in*   *vino veritas*
because there she was   because she was not alone   came dismal results

with wine-clear conscience   with burning barns and livestock   with no place to be
absented himself: forget the narrative mask: a life ended here
among changing plans   mocking goatherds all around   might as well kill me
tie me to a stake   honey on my intestines   man-eating bush ants
I'm dead already   dead since puberty looks like   note the tough guy grin
you'd think I'd have learned   for money you can have looks   how do you get it
they give it to you   instead of to someone else   you're feverish now

when did you first know   how much you're about to lose   not when you were eight
though that's a good year   saying to yourself *Never*   *this happy again*
seeing consciousness   the wall, the spotlights that brings   no it was later
loving another   but no matter how strongly   you can't keep that one
you can't keep that one   the fire burns its embers *in*   *vino* happiness

Pigeon through the tree

pigeon through the tree   slipped a letter in the slot   wrapped in a *black coat*
snow or butter melt   melts melting melted relax   it's not a school day
used a little *stage*   a teeny bird climbed the bark   glad I'm no ant-like
swaggering locals   *staggered* fell had to be held   already noticed
whisked the thin screen back   welcome to the greatest show   grippe she had they said

was a bit grippy   we still needed her nearby   we took turns nursing
sequenced pajamas   tenuous then worsening   infantilized me
so much for all that   fortunately free tickets   we just emerged here
look birds in the trees   what do they know about me   turns out no one cares
broken branch still stuck   in grass near a much-rung bell   *casts* his own shadow
little broken bits   poking in the root cellar   myths *mirrored* my mouth
cute little puppy   rototilled their garden plot   golden Oh wood bough

smacked she he the hand   found Everlife Plant in Lake   rested, had to pant
watch out for the Snake   does that still bother you now   it's been a year or more
the down log rots long   swept me off my feet a lot   helped a sour landing
about time he knocked   pointed her browser at me   very unhealthy
we've been unified   whoop-ti-do her strategy   one *boasts* a black cap

Boy on pedestal

boy on pedestal   literally atop it   where a statue'd be
acting out the part   shifting phantasmically   this as doubletake
my surrendering   Submerged Boy Emerging-là   (will Andrew grow up?)
the clockhand strikes light   along its length, to be *shine*   for just a second
the boy hops on down   the real statues are hidden   they'll be let out soon

the whole school's let out   off to guitar lessons and   TV shows, comics
to mild shoplifting   (went mostly for the candy)   seeking sex pictures
on the internet   pretend to be playing games   pretend about school
we're all so tortured   talk about moral vacuums   ripe for being led
curled up in leather   more popcorn by the TV   oh it's a great life
shouldn't have indulged   oh but it's all so comfy   get away with it
may we please keep it   pretty please Daddy it's so   cuddly and it's lost

turns into a cat   jungle cat and no mere lynx   a lion tiger
see this was a test   no I don't see nor do you   whispered to silence
nothing traveled far   you couldn't have overheard   you were in Quebec
I was in Jersey   how have we entwined ourselves   here on this same couch
you could be and are   my luck at nighttime I guess   be ready to run

She struck my trope hard

she struck my trope hard   I sacked her hegemony   she ate decentered
I repositioned   she went postcolonial,   neo-Freudian
I restacked Foucault   with lots of help from psycho-   analytical-
Sunday-at-the-park   reinventors of pseudo-   postdeconstruction
junkies, as they said   she tried neo-lesbian   hermeneutics but

by this time I'd gone   there was a soccer match on   from a German feed
of course it's still on   but I've something else to do   a rod in the fire
as they say is worth   two in the coldwater plunge   or chamberpot or
still raw just sitting   here as I was nothing wrong   nothing going on
found a solar pad   that buckles on the outside   for heating your shoes
but that was crazy   just a moment's invention   someone's stray daydream
that's all I'm made of   just a moment's invention   someone's stray daydream

snared out of nothing   returning there quick enough   but how will I eat
that's a Groucho line   she wants his arm to dinner   cleared his throaty throat
whose train arrived lately   the twist-fest had ended then   dust flew down the path
singing woodpeckers   a land of beautiful toads   I was dreaming then
I'd had too much drink   you could tell I didn't know   tried with your sister

Hunting for a tune

hunting for a tune   a flaring phrasal sequence   linearity
which a voice can catch   and likes to think it can catch   and still be brand new
like Plantagenet   descending to J. Genet   but gaining readers
we are more now now   no wonder we're living so   we're mostly living
success as species   wrecks respect your elders shtick   what's to respect *huh*?

I'm a placater   he kept praising his own stools   I just got edgy
my kiddo brother   I showed him how to get high   that was years ago
he's been dead before   before then I mean, not fact   it's mostly "friction"
we keep forgetting   so do you sick kid and all   buy some pyramids
forgotten "fern bars"   a whirlpool to down under   went as reverse birth
mainly they were gay   we shared the shiny dance floor   whatever makes gold
then they sucked in need   later I thought you had too   he counted it out

ordered three lobsters   as if the sea produced them   money on a myth
crippled by his back   amateur masseuse revenge   take a union card
never so bourgeois   son, look out for number one   let's study folklore
decimation friends   made so much noise chewing gum   mouth swollen with it
bunched it in his cheek   hey I've seen that on TV   did all I could do

Dodecahedrons

dodecahedrons   even icosahedrons   don't behave like Earths
but good as concept   for crafting a leather ball   lots of stitched panels
but as Earths — you'd step   from one flat plane to the next   more than culture shock
because there are rules   keeping imports to notions   nothing like I-beams
no TV sets no   generators no lumber   only ideas

and small stuff, neckties   stuffed baby animals, blush   mascara and such
each plane has money   but each has its own system   well one plane has none
they're barterers there   very few tourists can go   you can't bring much in
so you're not worth much   and the rule is you can't work   so, few stay the night
unless they find love   someone who'll marry them there   then they stay and work
the marriage bureaus   near the planar boundary   thrive as pleasure domes
real sex palaces   since that's what all can barter   for the hope of love

and if you marry   you go into the far woods   into the dark wilds
carve out your outposts   catch salmon wear beaver coats   the weather's nice-brisk
the life sensual   at noon that plane gets so hot   you worship naked
and sunbathe and love   singing hymns really singing   songs for the cosmos
being wonder-struck   being destined to die alone   though so full of love

Wild pigs hunt acorns

wild pigs hunt acorns   a jet breaks through consciousness   dogs there too, and birds
inside it's turmoil   no one sleeps with this lit night   the ground snouted through
mirrors laughing back   where sullen silver consents   the stats show rebounds
and percentages   at the first gap a cock crows   erasing so much
I'll buy that CD   each day the strike takes an hour   whirling on Earth's skin

eating from her lap   a 3-D figure of speech   glasses included
it's not all TIME and   MONEY but is for many   or so they'd believe
o come back my friends   o read the dried graffiti   o central casting
o shocking freedoms   will you wear mismatching clothes   he likes big cigars
instead of workouts   wise witches what will you say   brunt-bearing members
misunderstatements   we were set back many weeks   his pious tulips
his scrunched-up pug nose   the Santa diving outfits   that's a tight focus

widened your angle   picked her feet up high but still   can't escape the smudge
violence of her   hatred persistent as grass   creepgrass you can't kill
once it comes you move   burn the island behind you   leave on the last boat
sounds like a movie   of course there was an angle   she was an angel
her name was Engel   my grandfather's papergirl   I saw it on tape

Like cauliflower

like cauliflower   an interrupted outburst   in slow slow motion
as if still growing   manifesting a sharp wish   not so much *for* you
as to be near not   *you* this time so much as *then*   the time you dove in
the time you didn't   I could hardly either way   believe how pretty
the water was with   you in it and plunked me there   for no great reason

that was an instance   I couldn't raise the seatpole   no tools to be found
but you could still ride   yes I will have a third, thanks   but a bike's a bike
a horse is a horse   you still feel the wind talking   sometimes its music
unfolding like growth   expressing subliminals   those minor somethings
diminished sevenths   that seem to be expressive   not in the raw form
but in a thick stew   syrupy between soft chunks   and plump surprises
she said she wouldn't   but he found ways to make her   that's what it looked like

yes oregano   not very much normally   and fresh-ground pepper
wine if it's around   the rest assembles somehow   turnips and chick-peas
lentils and sausage   look what's happened we were nude   elegant Europe
Dubrovnik back when   I'll call it Angel Island   then I'm trudging home
a bursting bladder   weepy cruciform music   life fighting for life

The gears slip-sliding

the gears slip-sliding   that is (a) not years (b) gears   they slip when engaged
becoming useless   catch another engagement   not that you notice
you still pay the rent   just to different landlords   repairs *seem* slower
revenge of intent   you wanted me to be best   but what was harder
not sweating at night   *not forgetting the acorns*   such trashy gullies

our cute ambling duck   couldn't care less about us   we're his food machines
he little suspects   he's Christmas dinner this year   yes that was cru•el
sluiced and baffled it   the flood waters, rare this year   sorry — changed subject —
there was a norm there   'twixt you me and the flagpole   jumped a grasshopper
or a katydid   *Katy don't* the rest of that   strange green lacy wings
surprised by shoe creak   seems like the frontier to me   had to shoot Donkey
I love the first screw   said to be Archimedes   I don't like rumors

I don't like gossip   unless it's *really juicy*   found an old cello
unwrapped the sandwich   tidy little mess therein   threw away the most
flushed the pointers out   suppose you were Godzilla   floated on small boats
to blue Danube's end   back between the wars so bad   I'm sad to leave you
I hope you're OK   must have been a little stroke   no one's yet noticed

The only reason

the only reason   you don't know who I am is   you think I'm not you
tried a head series   tired of heads tried cardinals   messed up a sweet rhyme
explained a spondee   without ever hearing it   who cares what it <cod>
whenever she calls   there's a switchback on the way   collected beer mats
that's very good, that   whimpered when she went through there   amiable frogs

argued at dinner   not me, the man and woman   the woman question
/guess who took her side/   /once I thought women couldn't/   /now we ask, can men/
Topeka cellar   my grandmother's violets   her Christmas cactus
a prunish preserve   I review the parts of speech   they used to be prunes
they used to be plums   they used to be plum blossoms   they used to be seeds
pls. exoticize   abbrev. makes scor-   ing harder, yes no?
I called it *playground*   well really I said "*Spielplatz*"   oh they laughed so much

embedded discourse   imagine sixteen brackets   yes, pairs of brackets
it's really the speed   the appearance of challenge   hunt and then conquest
well look here I am   blood dripping off my fingers   dripping down my chin
me mighty hunter   grunt grunt got the girl grunt grunt   put food on table
squirted through puzzles   such a generous tumbler   /sensate odalisques/

Anna found me dark

Anna found me dark   she waved everyone off   PROBABLY VICIOUS
true I'm not so frank   true I have horrible dreams   certainly vicious
she came to the door   her breasts visible through net   her blouse not much blouse
spoke about her friend   a girl who liked being struck   by his belt let's say
was I to reach out   because I wanted to no   my girlfriend was there

a sophisticate,   probably *you* were vicious   Anna, you went on
collecting men then   decided boohoo not me   and my girlfriend too
who knew me wicked   and who knew me desperate   and knew me wasted
she went away too   there's a story that goes on   you'd find it obscure
chunks out of a life   whose cement looks like anger   subverted from when?
I was born this way   that must be the solution   the mortar I've got
for me to play with   to mold a life with alas   to watch ooze away

how to not be coy   how to not act shamefully   while dealing with shame
— any avoidance   acknowledges ignorance —   — thoughts not yet absorbed —
it's still a dark night   the hoped-for sunrise remote   the shouting stars taunt:
you'll never suck here   you won't be the thing I want   I won't help you out
you can sit and cry   'cause I'm the Mommy that's why   go ahead and die

You guessed broccoli

you guessed broccoli   but it was trade wars and strikes   variety shows
reverb entered in   then we had the broccoli   the room was served hot
a clever zipper   always closing in on us   not a nice waiter
he said "al dente"   in a different context   already noted
then the Boeing dipped   heard a frightening rumbling   they played with us, played

I like those red roofs   not the motel chain the tiles   real interlocked clay
a Delft ornament   tea trade subjugation ware   made them work the work
I've seen clay painters   quite a life if you start young   freaked by drier ground
there were embraces   I mean behind the Volvo   not that I would peek
let's stretch this out now   laying skins on then more skins   building up a face
burst through her garden   its drab triangular plot   you and him and him
can't trust those elders   holes blown right through the kleenex   so they were peeking

here's a soothing touch   excellent posture and tone   gracious me in bed
swimming doggedly   there's only one way to go   here's a snagging tooth
and a singing tough   whelped them all one at a time   they joked about stuff
which boomeranged back   like art nouveau in your time   freed to be brilliant
I touched each mushroom   it was a regal moment   there was not much else

ELEVEN

Light swirls down through glass

light swirls down through glass   patterning the desk, my hands   galaxies in space
that nebula-shape   dust storms against a background   perhaps just a ground
an almost frozen   swelling up within the sea   silent upswelling
then the boat swishes   a subtle portside twisting   and down down slumping
jolted starboard down   up silently swiftly up   to list port then back

lone speck on the sea   stormy winds and now the rain   will the craft survive
lips are getting thin   doubt, fear, nothing's been assuaged   the radio's on
we're ready to yell   not that it will should help come   we will or we won't
go over escape plans   no need for PFDs yet   not to that point yet
just a long way out   seas getting a bit heavy   lifeboats' moorings tight
a sudden sinking   jolting listing rising up   listing to starboard
the darkness lightens   sun reaches down in a haze   moirés in starbursts

its speed calculates   as it roars and sweeps (pale tropes)   through space beyond us
beyond these small words   not to be experienced   still, kind of pretty
as the light's pattern   is attractive and so still   on hands and keyboard
they've fixed the Hubble   (again) stuck new tools on it   made me think of it
and the seasickness/   uncertainty of being   in the midst of things

Blips and blebs in glass

blips and blebs in glass   distractions from what's *out* there   whatever's *in* here
not the medium   its idiosyncrasies   not sight but near-sight
cousins with insight   *wouldn't deny the poor worms*   paraphrase V. N.
who said we're *shining —*   *no matter how narrowly*   which helps dogs find us
that's speculation   and yes mirrors have them too   with the same pleasures

things start crowding up   hearing of a new vacuum   that things were wanted
to rush in to fill   the bushes pushed in all humped   looking neatly trimmed
a skeptic scarecrow   argued against a rumor   of things physical
and got himself in   as well as his notion (that   rhetorics need work)
fish kept slipping in   no good way to keep them out   besides they make food
firestarters got in   perhaps in the pockets of Scouts   but they brought smiles too
campfire memories   whole libraries rushed in but   lots of books fell down

a mewling black cat   was perhaps the first signal   this would take too long
the hikers were fine   then their suburbs came along   soon there's no room left
and cities want in   whole years of big life events   carnivals and deaths
and the frailties   my God the poor frailties   how could we go on
and the children's toys   even those meant for grown-ups   well we closed the gate

Hi there I'm new here

hi there I'm new here   say, did you just pick this up   wouldn't that be strange
quelle coincidence   I just bopped in, uh, by plane   to tell you the truth
I'm always nervous   I mean you know right at first   no biggie, just nerves
and not drinking, yuk   you know, with a couple drinks   *anyone*'s friendly
but I can't right now   nice of you to ask though, thanks   sure go help yourself

oh you're back — somehow   I was afraid you'd have gone   like most strangers do
they think lord knows what   I'm going to measure them?   I guess I could try!
walk up to someone,   say, "Excuse me, may I, uh,   you know, *measure* you?"
you're pretty funny   about now though don't you think   we know each other?
I mean well enough   we could try sitting down? there,   I'll tell a secret
no I won't *really*   you don't really want me to   give me some credit
I'll think something up   you can call it a secret   okay then here goes

no this isn't right   the chairs are in the wrong place   you see much too much
let's try right under   the punch table's tablecloth   these others won't care
they're preoccupied   look she's already *panting*   that's how it is though
see *this* is private   like I always say, private   in a public place
thanks, you've been so nice   you've made me feel right at home   I'll remember this

Approximated

approximated   not simulated not forged   the real thing but *slant*
or *squint* if that works   the whole farrow squintSquintSQUINT   little tails wiggling
if you want stink too   you'll have to find your own path   mine has been cleaned up
there've been some deer here   you can tell by all the spoor   I've seen no foxes
I don't know their scat   *don't know scat about foxes*   my *ascenseur* stopped

got out: the 4th floor   then was lost in cyberspace   how did I find you
wicked storms rough seas   blitzing ELECTRONS stormclouds   losing connection
then reconfigured   all is well the sun shines on   above these dumb clouds
we find the sand warm   the waves firm but not angry   we amuse the birds
which is amusing   in the next cove sea turtles   drag their egg cargo
out of the water   make a nice safe home for them   deliver and go
not so fast as that   not like our UPS say   colored the same though

you tongued a lip tune   made me forget my worries   your hands are SO SMOOTH
I forgot my plan   after all my strategy   had only one goal
to get me right here   and since here is where I — no   that's not yet complete
it won't full-circle   part of me I couldn't drop   (my clothes I could drop
and my credit cards)   your touch — to touch you — to find —   to go on from here —

Suppose the kid says

suppose the kid says   *screw you and your fucked-up world*   *I'm switching to drugs*
what would you then change?   a week's vacation won't do   what is it he wants?
"inner sense of worth"?   "social integration"? or   "individual
attention"? blah blah   maybe he's got a good plan   given the weirdness
beginning to end   of the whole what-we-know show   that lives this as us

or suppose he says   *I piss on your greedy world*   *I will be a monk*
or *I'm a Shaker*   thinking: slow group suicide   nice people I'm sure
what did Frank's dad say   back in old Assissi, say?   NOT *who gives a shit*
I'm sure he was pleased   one less kid to think about   pay tuition for
and beyond a doubt   Frank was clearly one strange bird   so it might work out
you still love 'em, though   that's what Bess said, though her son   *let his chances go*
in favor of kayaks   Outward Bound survival stuff   ice-climbing and dogs

it's almost correct   that we think others would do   just what we have done
were they "in our shoes,"   that's what Sartre says, but that skips   the wrong stuff we do
knowing that it's wrong   and should you discourage him   from seeking comfort
though that's so bourgeois?   you have to urge him to join   learn and get involved
you know, *you* should too   it's not time for the sidelines   that's just easier

Shadows sheathing ice

shadows sheathing ice   perspective tricks bouncing stairs   numbered among them
growing green formals   architecturally void   DIRTY dirty tricks
I'm a systems "frug"   yes you've got the WRONG NUMBER   his voice got number
but then who am I   a solar-powered snow probe   avalanche-warning
don't capitalize   the effects have been rumbles   by then it's too late

it was step-by-step   he looked into space and leapt   his balloon jiggled
no Biblical quotes   speaking of how things have changed   no Greek ones either
I heard her singing   she will always be singing   that's how small she was
so tucked into words   you think that's sweet but it's sad   giants so reduced
her true history   she was always fixing food   mopping floors washing
nagging the children   out shopping running errands   only ever once
she felt like singing   perfection of light that helped   freshly whitewashed stairs

I'm through with that hank   set it down pick another   many-jointed worm
frilled articulates   beautiful caterpillar   wrapping itself in
to metamorphose   you think that's sweet but it's sad   will express itself
into butterfly   it had to eat all those leaves   that's the price of ART
of the insect type   where *repetition makes* uh   uh *reputation*

So you won't get lost

so you won't get lost   there's been a review scheduled   for later tonight
the Basics at first   then the Overview-abstract   repeated Contents
in fact the whole Course   beginning with Chapter One   its brief Argument
Themes of Sentences   with Theorems and Evidence,   if you want Detail
also the Reviews   Questions at Chapter endings   even the Footnotes

thought just a shadow   the shaping of the subject   dancing beside us
while we're occupied   with being serious the   really funny stuff
a bit of a change   from how this has been treated   in most chronicles
or even novels   note that the schedule *requires*   tender compression
by which must be meant   that slight squeeze you will give me   when we once meet again
even now I'm drained   but I will be there myself   despite missing chess
you know, the TV?   exquisite commentary?   fertile with game plans?

you will hear it all   thinking you have heard it twice   once when you heard it
and that once before   when, as it made perfect sense,   you slept clear through it
that kind of sweet dream   you get in a reverie   in a public space
you smile with glazed eyes   there's someone looking at you   maybe one you'd want
you smile and can't see   as if it were planned that way   though something else was

That's a sad black cat

that's a sad black cat   an engine just started up   thinking about love
that's what's with that cat   another motor tooled by   bandanna magic
Sanskrit influence   wind in window sighing oh   riverbend reply
not seeming to leave   scenery staying the same   dockhands who were they
instead of leaving   it's your picture on the wall   swift lift through transit

checked all the Dadas   cornered the system-hungry   used crosswalks on time
found a stray missile   put it back there let's suppose   consistently rich
ran him off the road   get to that in a moment   not so many trees
not so many toots   he took and tooted and look   lo a star emerged
witches came later   little demons in his bed   under the privy
shameful to hide there   *gambrel* they sang, and *lintel*   had to take a loan
not that she's alone   there will *always* feel no way   there there you agree

exhausting soulmates   they're still making stars you know   right out there in space
(overheard bus talk)   that weirds me out man like wow   saw through fine crochet
each had a doily   talked with circularity   a great family
oily filigree   dimity persnickety   alms fertility
the things to play with   stacks of blocks to knock back down   *basso profundo*

Who's left now who loves

who's left now who loves   loves Rube Goldberg any more   whose wings flew him off
or vanes with two flaps   tunneling specious water   like bunting in golf
let him demonstrate   first a loud wind is required   note where the exits
the vent and waste pipes   a roof like a battleship   (wooden bottleship)
overextended   trussed out on a plank and broiled   (worked with Derrida)

a blot on the sun   all meant to both roast and peel   lordly viscountess
smothered in linen   a tiny stack of jetons   which neck of which woods
bulging through his fly   the air's alpine memories   thrown in a hot train
just more paperwork   always feels good to stretch out   don't eliminate
anti-Indian   graffiti-freaked i.e. marked   (*pansy freaked with jet*)
imbalanced onions   they never make Mexican   it takes long tweezers
many nights no dew   tried a bar called Neverland   eagles dine for free

important phone calls   tried out his wine cellular   pulled out his ear hair
smiling gardeners   stood by the sound barrier   scorched with an iron
certainly tempted   considered being tempted   they lose when you win
Alaska cousins   counted it twice to be sure   usually more
epithelium   able to vote but can't think   manipulated

No one *knows but me*

no one *knows but me*   grim stuff circulating here   what if he should fall
(what if he should fly)   what if your bones were THAT COLD   slid down frustrated
this drama thank you   their wingsound beat the bushes   as if new leaves fell
ever washing hands   noisy bird has flown the coop   spring interrupting
bought more insurance   used bread for sopping gravy   afraid of losing

nobody knows dreams   not comparing just bragging   I swim the islands
but me poverty   let's get you to a drive-through   veered to a side road
got out and walked off   the vandals got there so fast   like capitalists
gave his goods away   more people in dark trenchcoats   started wondering
hovering till shot   I'm going to ferry them   a joy in veiling
and in unveiling   coming along so nicely   bad Queen Bountiful
so to say Queen Bare   queen of the empty cupboard   whose dog whimpering

the trouble I've seen   getting soaked lost and taken   denied or ignored
bracelets for the clouds   you could do animations   where do you take me
for what mystery   admitted bevies of weeds   admitted feelings
then ate the results   those dandelions were fresh   I did not know uh
vegetarian   uh food was so uh uh uh   nutritious, he said

Life is not just words

life is not just words   as slavery was not just   force chains whips and rape
what else? *ask* the sky   *tell it* to the fleeing deer   *chart out* the moon's course
touch the one you love   take in the fresh salt-spray air   climb another hill
then *talk* about stocks   *compare* photo processes   *pay* your bills and weep
anniversaries   come and go but what sticks out   from the messy mass

how did we get here   someone must have been asleep   piped up with nonsense
somehow it fit with   the general brouhaha   which closed around it
plus our willingness   to cut each other some slack   which made us change course
slightly, subtly, for-   ever: for a long time now   nothing's as it was
curious but true   questions and quotes protect us   the wolves are waiting
it's as if they were   pictures of pet wolves today   the local paper
we expect bad dreams   each with its own Errant Knight   turned diabolic

you Tower of Strength   me Wandering Here and There   you are kind of cute
I see a pattern   another drama ends up   shelved as comedy
no one anointed   Master Spartan of all time   no one gets credit
I have to object   I'm going to claim the prize   let the marksmen fire
I'll chew gum always   let the socialites quiver   from the woods he comes

Saved by Gresham's law

saved by Gresham's law   lesser things acquire more worth   saved by final sprints
after sluggish starts   saved by landaus lemurs junks   pulled under by hoof
that one tree sways so   on this other the limbs sway   had the right of way
never meant to yield   beautiful yellow pickup   *carbonic, butyl*
tweezed it out of her   you mean teased it out of her   as for restaurants

confessed and ate it   he faked his suntan so what   belligerent apes
groomed in the Kremlin   whereas we don't have those sects   flipped his Bowie knife
its haft end hit first   still a couple of leaves left   (season you behold)
their pretty tiled stoves   conducive to coziness   felt like a hobbit
tenderest moleskin   scrambled his apprenticeship   weird names for molding
always sticking in   inevitably vulgar   could have said it fast
detected matter   followed Landsat's imaging   won't you trust science

I was red and sore   never had to guess blood types   neglected her stamps
stealthily added   helped hold the hot air balloon   after hang-gliding
yes that tie looks swell   and there are these socks you'll want   idle talk of souls
as perched on fences   no wonder the dog's barking   those foreign helmets
what does *rich* matter   it lowered for balancing   avulsed the sky off

"Can machines have souls?"

"can machines have souls?"   "only if people have them"   chit-chat at breakfast
we think we're funny   even as if quite profound   trained by deep thinkers
roused by poltergeists   echo Navajo wisdom   those dead spooks and rocks
her bivouac's next   produced festschrifts on diptychs   it was his problem
applied electrons   old single-keyboard organ   practice AND patience

had a holy day   an antique skeleton key   straight from the movies
her picture's around   weathered their laughter but changed   no longer so free
he thought she was good   he knew she excited him   they said she's a whore
her kiss dismissed him   swept him yanked him a new thing   most wonderful lips
on a little porch   tricycles and junk nearby   always a cold wind
left enlarged amazed   they're playing sex tricks on you   oh well wheeze hack shit
damn emphysema   buglers can call all morning   sift the green flocking

would you be mayor?   what, have to fix the graveyard?   I'm thinking volume
you're thinking item   we both still want a profit   worked in the system
was once a huge whale   reduced to bones on a beach   set up like a church
the great ribs arches   you could see things symbolized   in such a setting
or you could see bones   you could see all this from Mars   there would be a fee

Got stuck on a train

got stuck on a train   train got stuck in strike traffic   why they fight like this
part of a larger   meant to enrich some not all   no place left to go
look an outdoor store   more surfaces photographed   can't cut *them* all down
studly phone combat   moving beyond the hardware   slipping in behind
curved their blades for some   varnished mushrooms for a job   made celery shapes

wrote a limerick   oh she's a white volcano   something or Drano
throughout history   guide to spiritual spies   called a widow's walk
called a widow's peak   can't say her eyes are gentle   hers was golden red
secrets in plain view   thievery went unpunished   plumped up his pillow
had whole trout for lunch   the stupid thing is blabbing   where does the bus go
a knife pocked with rust   what kind of mystical fool   got stuck on a plane
my dream was on strike   the plane kept flying circles   radio contact

cable quality   need to have a digital   where it never rains
but you can see through   hurt himself poor guy shaving   lava called aa
another codeword   it will take five hundred years   factory for souls
that's what someone said   sure it might have been a joke   so what's happening
what's happening man   as Baraka used to say   *still at No Dough U?*

Ran out of spray paint

ran out of spray paint   cut it off before its rhyme   not yet *finiti*
graffiti dangling   that's just what this town is like   *tutt'interrupti*
magazines torn up   someone wanted the pictures   conversations split
people running off   too many one-eyed beggars   no one watching out
pea seeds in the hay   new potatoes fed to hogs   hogs kept much too long

no one thinks to check   they hired a latin teacher,   Garcia Marquez
who started over   with paint making signs for things   but they kicked him out
for not talking straight   despite his fondness for names   the job's vacant now
kids are on the hill   smoking grapevines it looks like   no place for coffee
not the corner store   and 7-11 left   Kroger's might have it
the grounds, but that's all   you'd need a percolator   but now you're getting
desperate sounds like   and I can't see why you're here   or should plan to stay

fine with me if you   just get the hell out of here   you get my meaning
your uppity ways   nothing good enough for you   making small folk small
we were fine before   old high-and-mighty you came   we're still fine thank you
there's a door up there   I'm going through it alone   no following me
good bye good riddance   we've had it with your kind here   *graffiti* my ass

Pundits on howdahs

pundits on howdahs   too bad I can't go that way   doomed to tourist class
not so much footroom   an occasional upgrade   but then normal's dull
I take exception   I was starting to agree   completely futile
those guys look stupid   arrogant on their high horse   that's right, elephant
we don't have to nod   we know what's on the telly   affected her growth

divided again   first, that smell: is it good or   I'm not sensitive
I sucked into it   old socks or a cake or fish   excellent baked fish
hard to get old socks   with a model make and year   rarer than that one
the French are standard   even their mosquitos' lengths   one centimeter,
2 in legend, 3   only when you dream them so   able to tease nerves
I'm unwrapping that   constant recursion to dreams   a lyric weakness
who keeps saying *love*   why am I smelling *their meal*   *this* revolts us all

I return the car   we avoided ideas   in their eerie space
above the machine   though chasing them down shows us   how we yearn to be
beyond the body   which we've waxed to be hairless   in case we can't leave
mainly we plug in   tape the good stuff on TV   make three rights one left
drive to store and job   WORLD IS, we just can't say so   (we can just say so)

Little bits hurting

little bits hurting   used his voice to push me push   thoughtflash on dead rose
got them to show at   had a strip show next door town   eventual live
flare from moon earthward   caught in a barge interview   a real humdinger
live minnows bucket   guys on street corner bravely   couldn't hear it well
and it was raining   (Brian Eno said, partly)   as music barely

hitting poles with things   had to stop stop the music   the bears stay away
hassle the beauty   believe that fun has begun   noised up my motor
village guys in town   town guys in city city   guys in villages
the cycle of guys   he belches she asks questions   motorcycles back
please rent this machine   tickled the raised underarms   tomorrow's day off
powered by fossils   melted and burned with top heat   motorcycles gone
working themselves up   don't remove cap until cold   maybe we should ask

sand pushes me down   pulls me down and the water   the shore birds awk awk
blown stalks of dune grass   insects fiercely upon me   plain sand aches life forms
recorded music   going the way all things go   a pseudo-Buddhist
got here nonetheless   emphatic integrity   faked at the same time
like most mannerists   relished disturbances more   likely too narrow

TWELVE

Others woke early

others woke early   despite the ruckus last night   intricate U-turns
returning songbirds   monuments for suicides   so imbricated
protected from rain   a simple chain-mail armor   partly overlapped
counting on grackles   they'll be building nests here soon   ate more camembert
designed by junior   the kids are back with their bikes   big from the winter

shocktroop serenade   wartime evacuations   LEAVE THE MANOR NOW
BURN IT AS YOU GO   *eliminate intimates*   things you will not share
wait for the last train   the new kids' parents will leave   new ones on the bench
male teachers naked   nothing abnormal-seeming   we wait a long time
there's a war nearby   we need the term underway   where is the damn train
one of us calls out,   *YOU TURKS WITH YOUR BRITCHES ON!*   immediately
our girls on the bench   young as they are, fifteen, start   taking their shorts off

exercised her right   unmarried but had the child   the child is Lena
who plays peek-a-boo   sucks her thumb when she's sleepy   likes pears, oranges
has a little bike   has to have her hair so short   or she'd pull it out
Sabine gets mad   from time to time at Lena   Lena cries it's sad
it's sad how often   my kids had to cry at me   we were so lonely

Flurried greennesses

flurried greennesses   caroms feeling ricochet   felling windowpanes
by now three outfoxed   it was gabled garbled wrong   oh but it went wide
my heart I think went   winds went divans harems went   one could hear the Stones
one could hear the stones   nice audience who clip-clopped   birds turning corners
fruity ruminants   in a digital question   Gorgonzola check

how I so slim sank   her view on royalty gums   nobility gums
who would chew Beech-Nut   splitting literary dings   left silverware there
interviewed a mulch   had to be buried outside   invented desire
is that possible   I'd hoped even sleazy real   climbed the lonely stairs
each one a lone one   nice cumulus belfry man   grew inside musing
mustering is one   mousketeering another   museum-going
another space view   the great defenestration   o Luther Luther

drank drams drop by drop   spliced with one about Dumas   wrinkling barograms
got a great close shave   extraneous sibling stuff   all your warts are gone
held ice dust roses   Frederick the Great played flute   or J. Q. Adams
or one called Redbeard   annihilating angel   a stack of barrels
taking walks daily   Jerusalem vacation   Quito in the news

Mixed it up with him

mixed it up with him   overwhelmed with redundance   then yanked the rug out
many clues make sense   underwent unique insight   once-in-a-lifetime
spotted illusion   vanished waterbird species   spotted it that way
as it jumped that way   seemed to be magic but no   perfectly seeming
they fan the smell here   a sliver a fine shadow   stamped blue on the haunch

can quarrel with cats   considerably sharper   sidereal tang
full and luscious moon   meant it to be so kindly   dairy barn haystack
what keeps us happy   a bit larger than just words   strewn this way and that
that's a clever wall   so bound ridiculously   ran away crumple
smell of bread lingers   dedicated it to me   it's getting later
it's a royal flush   grebe and ouzel and small girl   flirted with gravestones
more asphalt today   limited by opening   slipped her a package

had to feel locked out   brushed sand out for weeks and weeks   touching the bottom
easy to make names   calibrated repeaters   yanking the pad out
sprouted unwilling   waterbirds over breakers   covering itself
stark lines eroding   centuries of trees since then   thinking is caring
the limb imbedded   grandfather who died that way   one can't help styling

Seventeen hunters

seventeen hunters   seventeen dogs one rabbit   TWEET the dogs slink down
BANG the guns go off   hope no one has shot a dog   now and then lie low
think of a riddle   now solve it OFF-LINE come back   a space and a time
yellow sails and white   brilliantly produced firestorms   lined up for pancakes
got oatmeal instead   got immense clear mica panes   translucent not clear

polished his hubcaps   mirage of execution   wrote science fiction
hinted sexuals   an ivy climbs that slow oak   pretty confident
wrote them from Berlin   faithful in watching the news   wrenched the book away
well it's not whining   sea lions' mating beaches   and ate Mexican
never a dull slide   his toes cold his toes colder   when lost in story
trudged ever dimmer   I'd like a huge hole right here   surprise symphony
try to think what's like   a sitting-there striver-kid   hey kiddo be sharp

twirled or maybe squirmed   got back in their cars and pfft   enough going on
hey the eaten moth   stepped in the dark and fell down   scared the campers
scared them yet again   hey that was fun you wanna   wore out his word book
spicular surfaced   has to be a part of SPEECH   redundant wired in
signed where the stone was   it was here within the time   a handkerchief hat

Power-tamped it down

power-tamped it down   started with the next-to-last   rubbled the sidewalk
saw a personal   radio from his pickup   nasty mass of roots
years to garden that   took him years to garner that   he laid down his plow
buried outside it   suicide in the '20s   that's a breadwagon
rushing to keep from   it hurts but you'd better go   seemed smart-alecky

chased the geese around   you'd think on a golf course none   they move the corpses
had a hot broth pot   set it right on the table   talked about technique
demonstrated it   slice the meat and stuff real thin   skewer it then boil
then Ray bought that place   hacked a sunroof in which leaked   things fell off cliff-edge
puppies but the tales   hunted polar bears for glee   used high-tech weapons
aborigines   (switched continents) chased down   (another story)
kangaroos with old   Toyota Land Cruisers/ran   them down thunk dead ha

mended the wind chimes   in honor of Nepenthe   beautiful Big Sur
rebuilt them really   had to cut a new circle   (wood) where the chimes hang
rout a smooth shoulder   drill the five tiny cord holes   then make new (wood) vanes
depending from chimes   retie the nylon leaders   I've been putting off
haven't done a thing   saw seven wild boar (today)   and then three penned up

We regress by hand

we regress by hand   by tube by playing Scrabble   the fire is too hot
the complexity   more beautiful by the stream   so close was fractured
frightening screaming   build a suit to withstand it   seem to make it form
yet does yet chaos   beyond glass dials we tap   emissaries go
who can be trusted   one throwing fruit from the truck   throwing potatoes

and it's not the case   there's no stream of safe escape   no banjo escape
no kitchen escape   Dinah knows she's no escape   hey we're really free
I'll check my balloon   you find some binoculars   school's out! party time!
did you feel that wind   sounded like bouncing bobbies   pegleg Pegasus
monkeys in the clouds   the set for *Wizard of Oz*   too much realism
no that's what can't be   infantile triceratops   obsessive joke-joke
punched PgDn, chewed gum   *gedankenexperiments*   began to unwind

gaze implies *something*   losing stuff in cyberspace   buffalo: *HARD WORK*
reached under his seat   with a true philosopher   vigorous Cubist
I'm superstitious   if the TV repeats that   Thelonious Monk
can't they tell he's high   there's a certain point of view   might be time to change
reveille gumbo   nothing left to emphasize   you would be so nice

An almost music

an almost music   or little bursts of lots of   every which way
it just makes me proud   one part of such a species   let us pray hey hey
it's much more this way   their pilsner's pretty tasty   a world of ruses
I could but I won't   furl the sail drop the anchor   keep your glasses on
help as a turret   when help comes to your city   unhappy duck goose

a break is a break   later there'll be another   it's ice floe jumping
or surfing sort of   scored one hundred fifty five   that was in Scrabble
and it wasn't me   not surfing jumping to floes   oh here's a landing
that one shifted so   you heard of these eye wafers   nice little matches
definitely blond   but it wasn't human hair   now it's worse and worse
I have sinned, I guess   left his dictionary here   little derringer
swords in the closet   nudged because she was snoring   I'm erasing that

you tap a pencil   a prussian blue for next time   why powder the wigs
loved revolution   vulture beetle smith or dog   made you too angry
then in the back seat   have you not seen such a moon   the deal is free rent
turned out they twisted   asked who won he said he lost   it's confetti time
sociable kingpins   collected whelks more likely   Miami tinfoil

Harmonies in green

harmonies in green   skirted a conviction that   still must close the vent
Pnin perhaps more so   looked willing to run me down   brighter leaves of fall
imagine a scene   in-line skaters tinkering   manufactured one
breeze through my fingers   quick-stepped to the parking lot   branched here and then too
threw her violets   decided to think no more   his parents have gone

we're expendable   we try to convince ourselves   that we're not but shit
we're expendable   here the grass pushes leaves up   the leaves weigh back down
taking to jogging   here on the downslope sliding   demonstrated flair
flair's a flare's a fleur   a flayer's a difference   hello Suzanne G.
hello Penny M.   embodies alterity   whomped her till she sobbed
poor sad sick young child   had a hard time with posture   those ab crunches help
ran up the long stairs   wolves have made antelopes slim   echo corridor

heard childhood door chimes   where there was a clean foyer   when fractals began
discarded questions   slat bench, a closet with furs   you must pick a card
takes a little time   but doesn't need permission   butted in to say
they didn't seem pleased   the reason his news got lost   just a weak prophet
should have studied more   rhetoric I'm delighted   there's a big change here

It's kind of cheating

it's kind of cheating   if you're in love with someone   to say *they* make it
they must do the work   you can't really FEEL that way   It's Academic
you both know you're each   aggregating it for each   *syn* with plus *chron* time
what we're looking at   demolishing that mythos?   create more freedom?
let each go freely?   unhindered by attachment?   get rid of the mush?

YESses to all five   at the same time NOs to all   let more mush swarm in
a place where words whir   so beautifully aren't words   it's so funny, no?
we hear more music   than we can recognize as   this not well blended
that's what I'm good at   cat smile disappear -ing -ing   smiling irony
sexy ironing   right away the walls quiver   better start running
here's an overcoat   did you remember your keys   almost got stranded
did and on a beach   was it a bird or a leaf   can it make nonsense

can nonsense be made   these are serious green cars   these should have been sung
more of those green cares   used to want meaning one way   the house of cards way
bit ephemeral   but momentarily real   but don't any more
just the cards themselves   grotto forms cave forms farm forms   weeds & birds & clams
always desire forms   eternal love and lost it   Milk-Duds and previews

Put up a brave front

put up a brave front   painted stripes on his forehead   she used the back door
kept it from banging   what came next is that next came   to intercept →now←
she had her cycles   the kitchen help got angry   someone must be →wrong←
demoiselles du nuit   pornographers make them pay   nothing too Cubist
how to tempt a muse   to pretend-play with money   not that we don't care

just sitting here might   a little jagged morsel   it's not what they said
I won't be able   and that's stupid and morose   sun makes this happen
he's an old man now   they keep folding up the sets   your calm is a balm
can't keep the kids off   despite the oft-published rules   climbed high in Nepal
called a "false summit"   makes you wonder what to trust   not the connected
→affiliated←   whirl of Alaskan islands   covered the Dred Scott
law court, not justice   yielded to missing some things   first among equals

her throaty decline   the curtain falls she's agog   they called it a theft
bumpty-bumpty-bump   why should we always each reach   tactful traumatist
the screen is wider   she sounds like Gertrude Stein →so←   its width determines
an eerie gumption   howling noncomprehension   working the walkways
scraped past the sunset   rarely the first to know things   pulled a lemon down

Serially sung

serially sung   as you could be asked about   "This Is Just to Say"
namely its line count   so, well, does the title count   from which one unfolds
a world fin by fin   then da capo, showing off   the fan's quick pattern
a kind of series   ❑ exemplary ❑ I insist ❑   I'm going to sleep
always quieter   you might have met *cinnamon*   suffragette's tea set

patient: *I'm not real*   doctor: *don't think about it*   wanna go fishing?
where the waves beat white   the world's telling us ROCKY   the noise is scenic
rare gulls gather there   and at low tide harbor seals   mind where your boat goes
that had been a day   this showed every promise   then it sprang a leak
we started sliding   might try real mountain biking   here's a blue balloon
little bears lined up   but the grownups don't notice   on the window ledge
I cry in churches   apparently it's music   or the sheer yearning

sheer both clear and steep   consider yourself a bat   shrieking in a cave
no such thing as *drop*   no such thing as *fall* or *flail*   no such thing as *walk*
in Minnesota   no one cares if you write *Dream*   *Songs* so said one friend
groping with his death   they are disconnected things   the phone kept ringing
no one could answer   no one could get in the house   *care* what is this *care*

When you have random

when you have random   number generators you   can have random words
generated when   you have random words you can   generate random
ideas when you   think random ideas you   may wonder what you
have created you   may know for certain you've got   the answer for world
hunger or even   egoism or ambition   and then you may think

that you'll never think   in the grand old true way of   thought when it was new
and thinking grandly   seemed the only ambition   and then you may think
about the price of gas   or the thread size of that bolt   you need, to install
those barrel inserts   into the oak legs you've turned   for that set of shelves
you need so badly   so your study finally   will function so well
that you can start to   think about more central things   like whether and yes
and why there's such a   thing as depression in life   without noticing

the sloppy piles here   and there of papers and books   you ought to read or
give a reply to   without pulling others down   in the pit you're in
which Bob Dylan said   hoping for our applause and   then you start to think
about Kathy and   the kids and whether they'll check   the oil in the cars
and then you wonder   if there's not a thought which is   unthinkable like

Run for a long way

run for a long way   feel like you are being chased   hide in a garage
two rakes, of two kinds   the leaf rake will be no help   grab the heavy one
swing swing and hit hit   sculling in a fast river   faster and harder
going the wrong way   slipping a little farther   getting into trees
what's behind that beech   an arrow in the canoe   it just appeared there

a white band a red   fletched with gray white and yellow   steel head imbedded
smell of roast chestnuts   weird but it's really funny   a movie poster
The French Anchorman   some Jacques with Simone Beauvoir   you guess you'll go in
no one's in the booth   there's a woman with her back   the lights flash and smoke
a snake on the floor   a white band, a red, a grin   they all seem happy
the woman went in   you don't want to follow her   you're right beside her
she gives you the wig   that was going to happen   you've been carried now

comic book jungle   dark natives ears pierced with bones   a big stew pot (yours)
you have to choose now   you're awful solving riddles   it's that or the end
you get really mad   like your dad getting nasty   they let go of you
say it was a joke   you're still mad you call them names   you want to strike back
you're holding a snake   you have it threaten to bite   it circles, flares up —

Wanting a nice chat

wanting a nice chat   have to stand there patiently   then the bread truck comes
he's all business   we have to recite our needs   not much nourishment
scenes from village life   carry the vittles back home   it's all drab today
there's a virus here   we'll all recover and then   it will be like spring
the miracles leap   that the bread exists, the truck   makes you praise the Lord

Edmund Burke once wrote: *the glory of Europe is   extinguished* oh my
here's how glory works: it's not there, there's nothing there   then it's back again
each dust speck a gem   each gesture incredible   language amazing
language amusing   each gesture inadequate   the room's still not clean
shortstop's at the plate   there's a decisive moment   hey we won again
(maybe not Denver,   not Indianapolis)   or tennis players —
unaware of balls —   that's like thinking "my thumbnail"   you don't if yours works

you know the work's hard   hack and dig and hoe to plant   protect the seedlings
harvest and prepare   store some up for the winter   save some out for spring
working the worst land   why, do they have better land   I'll go over there
for myself I take   then I get a wife and kids   I must defend then
my cause is virtue   all *my* hard work is virtue   don't irritate me

Eleutheria

eleutheria   the school bus has brought the kids   dogs bark and cocks crow
he won't let her go   had enough of his braying   those days were biceps
prettily the swans   used the built-in wheels through town   a pencil's chewed top
lentil-turnip stew   freedom fighters dying there   torn newsflash fragments
bunched between giggles   he thought she had something good   to make him better

somnambulistic   stunned into brickwork nightmare   can't get out can't pee
speaking Greek to me   insisting she see my car   tied a thread around
rhomboidal *Gespräch*   the border between silence   and music though sounds
so democratized   it's not what's music it's how   you listen (John Cage)
(idea not words)   what do you mean by *dancing*   well you've read all that
too sick to push up   rode her funny bike through town   bell ringing at bumps
she felt adopted   she'd always make love that way   a grit-spitting man

cynics that's perhaps   a little west of Hopewell   saw him taking naps
a naugahyde couch   engraved him broken by fire   balanced with values
used it as ballast   in the days of smoky ships   still scarred from his fall
witched with memory   divided into counties   brightened when she smiled
creaked like a sailboat   *a new walk is a new walk*   a new egg's a joke

Round the ragged rocks

round the ragged rocks   *the ragged rascal ran* and   he'd strut through his Rs
his Ayrshire or true   Northumberland heritage   rolling on ❑ like those
Lake District fogs? ❑ no   I was there as a tourist   he was the farm boy
whose father was at   Pea Ridge where his nose was shot   but my mother said
her grandfather bent   stiff-legged every morning   to fasten his boots

maybe that was the   other of her grandfathers   with the hobnail boots
it happens Kathy's   great-granddad fought at Pea Ridge   on the other side
so it goes with life   time works wonders after all   Sandburg and Whitman
would have said *grass* but   I was afraid you'd mistake   what I was saying
not that saying *grass*   will mean, say, *marijuana*   consider yourself
likely strange reader   you can tell I might shift gears   any time and you
what is your strange bent   that you'd look at books like this   thinking what you knew

let me nuzzle in   can I call you "dear" reader?   and praise you really
the world is simple   you think it's arranged so that   it's always weaving
you're absolutely   right did I tell you that you   were so sweet to me
this morning you made   fresh coffee and had croissants   oranges and sun
you wore that *peignoir*   you'd found in my cabinet   I felt I'd come home

Then the author says

then the author says   "Here's where I'm going to say   what I really mean"
as if the pine trees   so casually brought in   disguised a forest
approached that crossing   considered it a crisis   you're so serious
it's OK to pause   but a pause can keep stretching   finally just went
well I feel just great   you know I almost drowned there   each step a traitor

just counting minutes   the field grasses have begun   a great big buzzing
in the bulrushes   wasn't a crossing per se   an intersection
busy 4-way stop   primed to take a crack at it   huge tankers lined up
have you squandered it   fierce dogs with a sense of fun   all named Cerberus
made a donation   made it three times your honor   I was one scared stiff
turns out laughing helps   in the computer version   they can lose their heads
though they spring to life   if you forget to lock up   went back to shoot them

dreaming at her desk   picture of a boy with book   the future's a book
the boy's potential   her potential, her future   close the book softly
turn computers off   unplug telephone and fax   take a nap curled up
Canary Islands   nice exotic kind of place   wake and walk outside
mockingbirds so soon   and tulips and daffodils   now we can go on

THIRTEEN

Should be plug-and-play

should be plug-and-play   an oversight a mistake   but if you had it
you could stick it in   if you had a place open   what are they saying
the power shuts down   skin feels tight, tingly, remote   smoking by the door
to change examples   of barriers of lost days   not examples though
enactments (rest here)   a playground; posed no problem   enormous whiskers

a group of scholars   staging a reenactment   of groups of scholars
there's Mendeleyev   hush stop pointing but there's BLAKE   and BURNS and BYRON
anthological   something happened what was it   current slipped its banks
zapped a stack of cows   delivered the frozen goods   do you miss ice cream
they're not whom I meant   magazine called *October*   *après* Derrida
if you paint you're proud   to be just a painter yes   color texture form
which materials   other ways to practice art   funny fakeries

that's an example   my deepest apologies   he just sees it so
of course she's your child   there was a *dissolute rake*   you can call me Ace
can't get that station   don't have that nice equipment   it's wrong to be mean
who's he talking to   I'd say let them register   she wore a tight sheath
Marlene herself   had had lots of body work   was maybe 90

Decided no way

decided no way   can't let this narrow bridge be   need a wider one
I've always been mad   having cars drive down my street   so I threw a brick
both my parents yelled   they punished me with a stool   I had to sit there
was it a dining room   how many rooms had that house?   I keep adding more
each time I go through   it's true he did remodel   things got different

it was my dad's fear   about bridge, kids, fast traffic   I wanted to help
I see it clearly   he was getting a new bridge   built by the city
me, a guerrilla   took the law in my own hands   my four-year-old hands
I wouldn't know this   except for their 60th   anniversary
celebration and   the books Dad made on us all   in his, a new bridge
which he'd lobbied for   then actually designed   in mine, other stuff
nothing about MY   war against thoughtless speeders   I *did* break his glass

lucky no one died   another way to say it   traffic wasn't bad
never moved too fast   scared that guy good though, his son   traumatized, teach him
there's a moral here   precisely what I had feared   edges lift elsewhere
as if belonging   to a narrative zone not   the one this points to
to this and others   those Diebenkorns — Ocean Park —   well that's different

Wore a personal

wore a personal   hung it right out there for all   removed their zippers
kept the tape running   well it was full of howlers   started lining up
now that you've got it   reduced once again to tears   a pro-magic bus
if the condom tears   tasted all pretty plastic   not without feeling
the press do their job   testing and probing and sly   agreed to come round

he missed the real work   at that moment he was fired   his drawings burned up
they kicked him often   dogs marked him as they walked by   could he recover
he had a face web   scarred here and there all over   he had a mind web
no one watched him try   obstacles and dependence   unhappy story
he died and gave up   what was the weight we carry   what do we drop then
when we place these stones   now he's been joined by others   now's a prisoner
in tulips love signs   I'll be missing oh bow wow   they talked as trash blew

impressive flood stage   her going aground refined   I love by pronouns
the machine stamps dies   an around-the-world checklist   three continents yet
four (Antarctica)   how will you respond to that   write three grants and see
they don't give sponges   at least not the little squares   I'd like a fondue
triggered a new spasm   a band to hold his thoughts in   a source before God

She sits down they talk

she sits down they talk   underwater tentacles   test how they each feel
the talk is of jobs   cities months spent lovers gone   they touch and slip off
each stands proud alone   can't be reduced to needs now   each goes but looks back
perhaps perhaps but   other plans already made   leaves are still blowing
won't be much longer   footsteps down the dark sidewalk   fade into the wind

I still have your book   opted for the shortened form   will return it soon
and I salute you   I miss you it's hard to say   well hard to own then
plays with a twist tie   the falls at Lodore were sweet   a positive lean
came down from way up   trees and green and rocks hurrah   played and didn't fall
easily jealous   as for what you can take from   sure it's postmodern
a labelling bee   that's the MLA for you   like a quilting bee
not a honey bee   aw that was kinda touching   you mean mawk mawk mawk

it was on a dare   the true Cain-Abel event   Cain said bet you can't
and Abel couldn't   you can see it all the time   speeding cars won't yield
likes to find new roots   how about *wood pussy* for   "skunk"? that feels antique
(1899)   I will do illegal acts   she hates her own hair
others hate their skin   I'm kind of tired that's OK   a whiff of knowledge

Thyroids and Dante

thyroids and Dante   where the red carpet comes from   white wine or water
John Deere headquarters   what French school kids do at lunch   please sit on the floor
Army Museum   virtually an artist   Blake "good" at music
write dirty poems   why hog the whole blanket stack   turn the fan on/off
photos from TV   *Feu er Pau se* for instance   ends in empty rooms

around a campfire   ceremonies exhausted   learned it from father
big traffic island   confusing to commuters   pneumatic weapon
backpacks on blue squares   problems with technology   did you understand
so they were involved   Pushkin's cult can't be explained   will it come about
still know him by heart   yes when I was seventeen   quoted some Cummings
or Canadian   please don't set glasses on books   drawings of fabrics
photographed my friends   transformed them into plastic   Christo a master

I need a hobby   his leg kept falling asleep   have another glass
her red leather pants   brought Moses in a basket   a press conference
war in the Balkans   for him "Birches" the best one   read a different
end of their broadcast   carry the wounded away   in the front-loader
green with big red knobs   kids on bikes played on it too   park lined with billboards

Stepped into his life

stepped into his life   wrote back saying be wary   we never got it
got a TV show   people making stone-age tools   say a stone-blade axe
then chopping a log   using only bones and stones   so we did get here
not just a word dream   literate myth-creation   the one that says words
that words are the end   and the beginning that words   leave the gate closed, thanks

what's this Sandy Legs   you were just telling about   where the fat cook lived
climbed then to grandeur   ugly vocabulary   no the words are sweet
first barrel cactus   then bowed and produced rabbits   which flew off in scarves
leaving their daughter   right there as a magician   spirochete in form
freighted with kleenex   the first huge house flies of spring   crummy conditions
manipulated   had his dancing strings pulled by   wolves hiding in trees
made it back to base   shifting lights and wind volumes   peppermint candy

almost didn't send   used screws less and glue joints more   the next world congress
Jeunesses Musicales   Canada resurfaces   they'll find the church dark
many strips and stripes   crawled through many museums   there now in swimsuits
no there's a light on   time to learn the catechism   whatever otters
stepped out got blinded   you don't have to explain it   came back from a walk

Not their thickening

not their thickening   late-night visits about love   not the silhouettes
seeking high platforms   almost all the trees will leave   enviro-friendly
I am determined   none shall be more zero than   paper penises
already unpacked   the burden of IRON MAN   if they had caught him
smart patient daring   he could have dated the nurse   escaped and revenged

you mix with people   you get their wig diseases   scrambled a message
no but it looked like   happy childhood with cream puffs   and punched to the grass
redundant commands   launched the helpless boat sideways   kids do your lessons
retouch your pink spots   a multi-dollar bargain   made it, and kept it
it won't be *random*   hosting lingerie parties   the way I used to
back on the ropes course   they'll say, "he was sincere, eh?"   his skittered across
there he was in three   suppose the polish wears off   found *nidi* in it

rain and car coming   he *could* have dated the nurse   but never smelled it
the puny forest   these beautiful rugs to sell   these terrific pearls
what a time to live   they say SELENIUM now   had to be polite
they thought she liked to   they sure wouldn't have made her   not my good buddies
here's where what's what's THAT   we keep incredibly young   did a round-about

Yes Grandma Moses

yes Grandma Moses   no Englebert Humperdinck   yes Louis Pasteur
Edmund Hillary   Rodgers and Hammerstein   no Pierre Bonnard
no William Burroughs   yes Whitehead Russell and Ayer   no Jung yes Buber
no Annie Oakley   no Orson Welles no H. G.   Wells yes Jane Austen
yes Superwoman   yes Laura Ingalls Wilder   no Che Guevara

yes George Washington   no Catherine yes Peter   no Henry Adams
yes Howdy Doody   no Paul yes King David yes   Amos Micah Ruth
no Juliet Lowe   no Julia Howe no Marx   yes Homer Sappho
yes Buster Keaton   yes Captain Smith no Cortes   yes Abelard yes
Héloïse yes Maid   Marian yes Robin Hood   Samuel Clemens
no Garibaldi   yes Rembrandt van Rijn yes Ernst   Barlach no Huysmans
yes Popeye Shakespeare   Duchamp Bertolt Brecht yes Yeats   no Ibsen yes Joyce

no Molière yes Donne   no Spinoza no Pushkin   no Genghis Khan yes
de Sade yes Rèage   no Christopher Columbus   yes Jeffers yes Freud
no Derrida yes   the Flintstones yes B. Franklin   no Perry Como
no Einstein Woody   Woodpecker no Raquel Welch   yes Fellini yes
Sophia Loren   no John Quincy Adams yes   Bach Pollock Milton

Two black cats hunting

two black cats hunting   one like a note on the grass   lined with tree shadows
in and out of stripes   the other always partly   hidden by grass stalks
hedge bustling with birds   clear cool sunny almost spring   after rainy days
cooping us all up   hunters of idle moments   more rain predicted
they don't need to know   they act on that basis now   oh she has a mole

no one would buy one   they were trying to make points   with a sense of style
theirs being all style   unclear how it future-fits   the basic structures
the big difference   tetrasomething, aspirin   that makes the future
to be so spread out   the long country loneliness   *I*'m not redundant
and in any case   as if it meant the same thing   *I*'m self-sufficient
I don't belong there   or to them who are legion   it's a New World thing
if you know New York   they're still provincial and proud   even in high school

distressed, distended   dark night of the dream machine   who got their service
then made a wrong turn   grasses and reeds in a vase   fought against a chill
assumed a standard   who else empties the lint trap   she knew what and what
it spread out like farms   there's a skilled painter with us   made tape recordings
sometimes a sidewalk   a jet at the speed of sound   felt her sonic boom

First a few held back

first a few held back   just a moment's refraining   but it was enough
others broke away   behind whom the next held up   they reconsidered
saw a chance out left   went off in that direction   subsequently swarms
stumbled at Point Choice   some twisted forward others   split right or for home
resumed as magic   the long gone going going   some of them not all

she thought he teased her   he had never teased before   others must have though
we're sophisticated   drink tea in snazzy tearooms   street repairs outside
pavement saw dust cloud   the look on an angry face   the pay's good I guess
but it's not enough   if you want to be elsewhere   the Riviera
like in this Matisse   where light is a window space   dark is floor and wall
colors amuse us   her tea is red yours is green   mine wears a top hat
kicks a ball along   it has to do with patience   his table would fall

play reaches the point   well-tutored portfolios   matched or well-balanced
thrown out of kilter   (no etymon) to swerve off   one room of old jokes
toothpaste on the floor   a place where you order drinks   you never get served
your house remodelled   glass pyramids in the lawn   the royalty theme
Tattoo Festival   gift shop right by the photos   look we were so small

Unlucky thirteens

unlucky thirteens   slowed and ground to a near-halt   it's not *how you feel*
that's bad when you're sick   it's *how you feel about things*   that's an old saying
seems to have lost spice   getting from its first world here   or here's too complex
not as a structure   as a many-sided mass   as fireworks and smoke
to get to the heart   origination-belief   things we used to say

found a little fear   I'm raising my hand a test   you might call on me
have to hope you don't   feeling dorky-defensive   getting away with
but I can drop that   look I can stand up leap up   the old way was fear
will you see through me   the new way is transparent   not unconflicted
that's not what I meant   there's nothing clear about it   it's just that it moves
it moves in a space   it enjoys moving, that sense   and it's not a pose
like a pose but not   not saying *look at me here*   saying *let's storm on*

last year there were swans   this year we have to be swans   that's the difference
those from years gone by   they're mythic and marvellous   can't begrudge them that
we need grit to live   a little cracked corn, and grit   little bits of sand
I like shiny things   and I like smooth warm dark things   I'm a weather vane
I'm a rooster-doo   I flap my wings till dust blows   a tornado man

Viewed from a high rise

viewed from a high rise   people act just like puppies   ants or statistics
disappear to flow   the water stuff through surf rocks   hydraulic jetted
eroding and gone   then the vision's plain again   heavenly-empty
if you don't do that   don't summarize and negate   then you see too much
the boy and the girl   daffy all the way from school   anyone can see

then the full thrust thrust   for it's from each corner wind   bring you the latest
even before that   grimace and grin as they wish   each one no more room
got to fill his cup   let's get into those leggings   ruins just left there
torn moans and bleeding   called their rape *systematic*   yes it makes no sense
went to all that work   had to go alone both ways   in wind and weather
macaroni here   sorry guys that's what we got   stop your whimpering
go on and be sick   can't you tell I've had enough   now sit down shut up

a lot of extra   with the headaches and back pains   knees ankles and hands
scrubbing's all the same   go to church serve on juries   traffic tied in knots
jokers all have phones   push the wrecks aside plow on   don't forget the clothes
at the new cleaners   oh we're going out tonight   get all gussied up
listen to his jokes   I never get to have jokes   a polite coughing

Makes odd hairs shine back

makes odd hairs shine back   little blue juncos hop through   another school bus
lo the round shadows   lengthened into huts of shade   once we had a king
warmed by the brick wall   waiting for him to sing new   slipping in with news
not a mockingbird   then a little ditch digger   keeping few secrets
its opening hour   indifferent to your wants   burns unhappily

on the scale of things   that time of the tourist year   the last few swing by
there goes another   transit numbs the emotions   simply defensive
won't let the brakes off   there's a hazy problem here   would it hurt too much
I can take that risk   no I'm chicken I won't please   threatened by money
incurably so   against the pale *sky* the clouds   not much beauty loose
places it escapes   like geysers at Yellowstone   blows you away ha
oh we're whirling down   a solar experience   singing woodpeckers

solitary bass   they ribbed him because because   they'd won the prizes
he went to the park   arpeggiated for them   marched back and gleeful
hang up the phone NOW   another tries a cello   I guess you're allowed
sadly sought her love   rare mother's love unstinting   never truly so
but kept from loving   should try harder as lover   don't expect, make it

POEM FOR READING

POEM FOR READING: you're bewildered for instance   how can you relax
the world wants so much   hey it's Thursday, ten o'clock   that TV show's on
they walk through stories   they walk through major issues   moral shortcomings
you feel better now   most of the characters lived   some gained others lost
we saw them try things   no one's much better than us   so we'll keep playing

paying off the Dodge   drinking mounds of Coke and Bud   insured by the Rock
a moment's embrace   feeling *communal*'s solace   story's great beauty
we pretend so well   a role connects to a life   roles make sense of life
if you know yours well   just as problems can't be solved   until we see them
I think I've been gypped   I get really into it   then it disappears
I wish I lived there   in that TV show I mean   problems I could solve
not like here no sir   trying to keep things moving   JUST SAY THE ANSWER

tolerate my pitch   (even this which talks too much)   here's what you will get
an aerated field   words in groups of syllables   interruptedness
irruptive slyness   breathy considerations   (here's what five is like)
lots of little plots   at least the names of concepts   not truly random
therefore expressive   (this is a group of seven)   in an as-is way

Man poised with mattock

man poised with mattock   hnh HUAH ouh what have we here   this root runs from there
nnhn HUAH uohh big stone   this goes over that then down   must pry this loose first
ungh ungh unGH what now   this one's like a steel cable   try over here then
no with the shovel   clear this loose stuff off the top   lssht lssht uhnd and KNK
in the wheelbarrow   a broken open quartz rock   seemed so dull round brown

had to fracture it   to find its *inner beauty*   no and yes to that
it's just more star junk   like the rest of us and fine   when round and dull brown
the fresh-to-light break   surface never seen before   also fine star junk
it's the surprise there   well where was I with these roots   there's the big momma
nnhn hnh HUAH huh there   came apart like soft butter   must be rotted out
yes this young one here   got round and strangled it there   maple suicide
nhn nhn HUAH uhn yes   now we've got something to show   big hole in the ground

lssht uhd SLNK and toss   root chunks rotted or not off   by the plastic bags
lsst dhuh KNK loosened   worn-out soil from between roots   find the next tangle
nhhn HUAH ouh nnhn HUAH   ouh nhhn hnh HUAH ouh all right   any secrets here?
there's a millipede   sorry pal you'll have to run   gotta move this dirt
lsst lsst SKNK lsst KNK   time to haul the wheelbarrow   out back and dump it

Messed with exhibits

messed with exhibits   is how I've always done it   picked until it clicks
little this and that   pasted in the news of boar   crossed out *wild music*
a comfy old coat   just before getting worn out   still respectable
not for that reason   still functional so don't waste   keep focused higher
but adjustable   higher being relative   and fiercer than that

a footnote writer   occupational instinct   mistrusted statements
acted so normal   who lives by collage dies by   a John Deere loader
number one fifty   series B noted back when   on a Berkeley street
or try excision   the context of her worry   we might spill things there
we might ruin them   Dear Reader: not to worry   sung in Las Vegas
a drunk on a bus   DON'T WORRY BE HAPPY from   a pop song back then
not Monte Carlo   why must you always compare   your attention please

lined up on post-its   executed them quickly   threw away his notes
then lost the results   he had to start all over   oh what a dry saint
hire them and fire them   it meant divorce but what choice   falsely thought Greenland
messed with his helix   liked them with low-grade fevers   then things start to slide
shingles flapping off   older layers of billboard   last month's announcements

Nothing like the soaps

nothing like the soaps   the Titanic meets boredom   what old hands you have
Grandma said the girl   how can they learn us by name   we are the mushrooms
we're invincible   no we're horribly ugly   we watched them inject
dogs on an errand   planes spending the day on wheels   ducks scared to be ducks
intuit the rules   a couple more steps is all   you fall or it falls

eat my loveliness   you understand his bracket   golfer's handicap
employed his brother   trained as a historian   didn't have the math
learning to skydive   made him eat an onion raw   in an easement then
in a light derby   photon A on the inside   photon B up close
burning my bacon   autobiographical   just an appearance
like Hitchcock you know   *autograph it for you son?*   *I'll scuff it for free*
sure we've missed the sparks   exciting when lovers fight   a potato truck

did she take a tip   slips right on over those posts   then the printer works
consumer-level   i.e. small-time merchandise   when the old cook left
it's the big powers   would never have worn make-up   stayed home and got stung
bivouacked beside   since it was a free country   distracted by voice
guided by voices   up-and-down free wandering   along the cowpaths

FOURTEEN

What else but fireworks

what else but fireworks   that disturbance painted there   beside the church dome
or is that REALLY   just a large onion dropped there   those blocks like houses
it's sad days for Ralph   Sabine's with another   who's not onto Ralph
what would H. James say   keep your weapons well hidden   no these are grownups
bulls too old to fight   those birds must nest somewhere there   twigs too thick to see

still uncommitted   there are three of them hopping   all around in there
as for history   we will rewrite to the max   as they would do us
out in the fir wood   hoofprints in the soft sand mush   deer feed, then leap off
not the *sounds* I make   the *motion I make* making   cello sounds NOT *as*
girls on a guy's board   one sits the other pushes   they corner and tire
Pope wrote verse essays   Bernstein *et al.* came later   opaque-ish unrhymed
well we do get mad   if asked to read a poem   on writing poems

I dream of mummies   real ones but not frightening   there's a mouse in here
they look like they feel   I think I'd like to be one   or go skyjumping
the farmer's doctors   the three of them couldn't say   each named a disease
at nightfall closed buds   shadowed on the wall then blurred   into all-shadow
the glory of Greece   spike flowers by marble steps   dust, light, goat-bell chime

Over here shouting

over here shouting   quickly scrambling for cover   shouting then scrambling
next time up a tree   yes that suffices the bark   crotch footrests/bough stools
then down to a swamp   gloomy slitherings no wind   dank heat and green stench
a city bus stop   *only reason we're here is   we got no choices*
overdetermined: explains but doesn't excuse: there *are* things to do

first just sign here please   soon you'll get your desktop toy   your choice: rolling spring
or concealing blocks   and we've pocket toys for men   bracelets for women
for those not desk-bound   you'd never guess what we find   guys wearing bracelets
gals finger-fiddling   what is the analysis   people like to trade
love gifts most likely   correlate with birth date rates   might be a good thing
might be a good *ting*   *a ling* a lillibuloo   Irish pipe whistlers
dispelled decision   smacking more of the good life   smacking it tender

sure n if it's me   yr wantin mister I says   you'll watch yr manners
not quite a white swan   disguised a satellite dish   its voluble snow
hey they launch rockets   virtual's a sexy word   that was a picture
of a real blast-off   play laser tag for a thrill   you get these sharp vests
wired to a machine   you go ray-blast each other   when you're hit you're hit

15,000,000 kites

15,000,000 kites   stranded stuck in the world's trees   weathered broken torn
lots of loss left there   lots of little hands that slipped   big ha-ha March winds
some, you can get down   or play with this idea   durable, lightweight
meanwhile I'm hung *up*   finding *rips* in the canvas   *gaps* or pressure points
a fiddling with rings   I feel like spending zeros   it got cold, offhand

don't call me selfish   I said, DON'T CALL ME SELFISH   look at you yourself
whose freedom is this   go to the Penny Market   stroll along Sundays
a consciousness-net   catches some lets the rest go   not the bright searchlight
though that's excellent   roll it right over and gawk   they're in but they're out
lots of apartments   each a little different   this then digitized
enumerated   encrypted as inscription   start where you want to
not like a crossword   games have traps and obstacles   THIS IS NOT A TEST

not mind quality   climbed in and out of troikas   testing the bottom
mainly sludge so far   which is what we expected   in a this-like lake
elevation shifts   often dramatic declines   or alternate mounds
the hit-and-miss type   it's enough if you drive well   torque down the lug nuts
yes alternately   they were friends with deference   decriminalized

Cut a fringe for fun

cut a fringe for fun   rented a car with dark glass   kept trying new drugs
dancing loud music   incense soft slow music too   waiting for sunbursts
drew sunbursts instead   more original magic   walked past the doctor's
found the old churchyard   folks who've been dead quite a while   can't read the dates now
what's that clam shell mean   masticating assisted   *warum so dunkel*

wrote a little porn   excellent exercise plan   things taste so strange
not meant as a joke   tested the limits of it   tried the fit of it
found the hang of it   then put it through its paces   happened to see it
couldn't deny it   pushed it hard and beat it up   it made excuses
it had a birthday   it had never been happy   it counted dully
tried to help it out   developed a thing for it   a thing hung from it
it was divided   between it and the other   I couldn't find it

at the lake, dry reeds   a natural retraction   ghosted on radar
the door at the top   semicircular staircase   bad dreams about keys
circumspect wrestlers   sweating fleshed against sweating   needed a long break
made great photographs   thrown out the magic press door   hit the pool of moss
came back so briefly   an appearance of gunfire   must be the old news

A vase with grasses

a vase with grasses   pale olive-colored glass vase   nine regular rings
narrows at the top   could be used as a tumbler   with reeds and grasses
decorator style   alleged link past glass windows   acknowledge organs
which went responsive   on or before March 1st say   walked to the wallboard
removed old staples   walked back to middle of room   repeated a dance

repeating a glance   they accepted his story   not their magazine
just accepted it   as if it were authentic   children slaloming
around the gravestones   accepting them as meant there   help keep us limber
try my martini   opening my arms so wide   mean to do a rock
no back a minute   I *ACCEPT* what you're saying   there *WERE* martinis
these gravestones *ARE* rocks   one loop keeps going this way   you've fallen asleep
there's no other loop   a continual branching   an outbranchingness

worms have their own thoughts   expressed as desire and fear   food water sun bird
that's the fear of death   we couldn't deal with just that   we spread ours around
like butter on bread   everything shares a bit   whenever "you" go
"I" feel horrible   you have to read that yourself   grow to love it all
grow to love it all   grow to love it, love it, love   it all, all, all, all

I see my life now

I see my life now   flushing ten deer from near woods   on across the path
[a bird visitor   hopped up on my window ledge   stretched himself SO high
thinking *what's in THERE?*   I clapped my hands, the motion   not to make a sound:
timely intruder]   they crossed the sandy path then   through woods and across
another pathway   into woods for good, leaving   anxious footprints there

a life of panic   though the deer don't really lose   one part of the woods
is much like the rest   while to attack narrative   because we're swallowed
up by narrative   or by getting things to fit   buying packaging
for example not   what we need but what we're taught   to believe we need
so we feel just fine   unalarmed by what happens   in the world that brings
us to think all's well   when so much is badly screwed   people and the earth
our anesthesia   but to throw narrative out   would mangle the point

plus we couldn't read   William Carlos Williams, say;   eventually
we couldn't read AT   ALL; that is why would we, hey?   that's why I let it
creep around through here   jumping from clump to clump or   taking you over
which you're also grate-   ful for, a break from being   bumped around so much
though I do want you   (afraid I do) to feel these   woods faced to your face

Held in a balance

held in a balance   the right pan, friendly goodness   the left, snappy cool
it's a *purr*-fect match   peaceable kingdom ad from   animal rights folks
the gnomon's precise   lays it right on two o'clock   not much of a clock
designed an igloo   nice place for the kids to play   but a skunk moved in
left her heartstrings bare   guys kept lighting her up high   torch her and move on

she would still be bare   she'd act worn-out for pity   she'd be protected
again neglected   well that's when I stopped caring   sad to admit it
tired of Alaska   tired of the long winter night   the myth and the tale
they rigged a jury   no, they jury-rigged a thing   like a come-along
examples of love: make-up, hair color, nice tights   assorted condoms
examples of love: croissants, chocolate sauce, cream   cozy comfy room
examples of love: Russian, Abyssinian   little parts of you

concealed in lockets   as amulets on armbands   clipped one of the locks
wrecked the whole canal   took weeks to mend properly   loads and loads got ruined
mules got fat on grass   and not having work to do   wrote off about it
got a job on staff   got a big Teapot Dome lead   made a rep on pain
scummy surface yuk   had to go in for the corpse   under one same sun

Formidable skill

formidable skill   finding new ways to skin cats   not much practiced now
not in my circle   we're only figuratives   not a real circle
not skinning real cats   though if we had to we could   with our rust-proof knives
so we're entitled   to benefit from a glow   whose source we can't see
with a kind of faith   which feels rational and right   though strangely wobbly

which was at the time   of a great general sense   of stout well-being
so that the query   could be put off a long time   which was the reason
at least probably   that we never looked around   fretting over things
even that wobble   which was at first a small throb   in a pinkie vein
so to speak but grew   to a thing we had to see   trees bending bending
so to speak and broke   but that's what it took to see   to make us stop to see
we'd been fretting *here*   we'd missed seeing problems *there*   WE COULDN'T SKIN CATS

too gross to think of   there was no time for a school   no one could teach us
our cats were sacred   we'd turned into Egyptians   without mummy skill
this is history   *old hat* by now — we were saved   by modifying
the adage to us: *more than one way to feed cats*   it was that simple
it was literal   and helped keep us emphatic   in our homely tropes

They come easier

they come easier   Miralda surely told you   when they drift away
she can study eyes   that's more than anyone should   not that you'd asked me
I don't need to see   what else can they do with me   except fantasize
what's it now big boy   that's all I have to ask them   they point or mutter
or maybe they've got   a list stored up they're keeping   to bring down on me

it doesn't take long   for the stuff to slip from them   spurting and then ooze
they knew they'd won me   when we got the money straight   that I'd be willing
I got no problems   got no fucked moral scruples   delaying takes time
and I don't waste time   I won't look this good for long   my peak earning years
and yes I could die   like any poor motherfuck   any sec I'm here
but that's just dead meat   that's just already dead meat   no point worrying
and I've got a fuse   things start dragging or get weird   there's a mean bitch near

I've gotten away   there's been a few times I've run   left my shoes behind
dressed on the way out   knowing the muscleman there   would protect himself
before he chased me   he'd already done his stuff   what we agreed to
was getting greedy   I've never blamed anyone   fantasies are mean
like Cinderella   a mean dream to give a girl   you have to leave it

Expecting it here

expecting it here   on his knees in an instant   wail delivery
the broader context   hawk hanging in field-edge wind   as commentary
exploding beside   hung on the lip of the hole   when it sank they cheered
mostly they plotted   how to squeeze in a haircut   where to meet for lunch
of course things went wrong   pleasure of things working out   what things those things oh

no dim religion   borrowed purple paperclips   prepared mandalas
gave each a number   so much waiting in the dust   tedious artwork
snuffling and grunting   overheated the firebox   seemed so devious
well it was right there   it was a mountain brook bank   no clay deposits
that was another   equally devout counties   which came out backwards
we saw them scrambling   every night they washed socks   naturally then
despite the ringing   ice halos round the pebbles   fundamental air

in a sense within   they never came back from that   lost beyond bluestem
easy to topple   already beetle-ceded   hollowed from within
unproven mélange   *which witch spit Swiss Miss death wish*   suicide parade
couldn't stand the smell   made them make a ring and smile   disparate men's stores
flapped its ailerons   not an intellectual   approach navigates

After my haircut

after my haircut   shedding trim-ends left and right   caught as they dangle
brush all of them off   fighting the Good Fight with fire   learned it and forgot
learning forgetting   what they *won't* absorb *won't* care   *won't* like their stylists
crimped all those pages   magnificent magmagnet   I couldn't read that
the way the light skipped   like a spot of yellow trash   field   visualized

got a deal on it   exploded into success   franchises, trademarks
met a need we'd had   no one else had recognized   textbook example
truly surrendered   meaning no guns left at home   didn't feel beaten
so goddamn stubborn   it'll seem to go faster   rocks will tell a tale
their odd alphabet   based on an Arabic frame   arranged vertical
can't read the busses   so dry you don't feel too cold   western glacier fields
were made to change it   overloaded memory   ended pallid truce

came out with new ones   had them sharpened month by month   a buying club thing
fresh air of kindness   breathed it deeply, longingly   hoped to discover
body's deep cauldron   not just a stew for gluttons   overcharged its seams
energy roamed through   overcame with touch and smile   tamed and nursed to health
there were lovers freed   by the idea of sand   all-once-together

We looked at the wind

we looked at the wind   it stood resolute and dark   the sea was in it
and ice fields beyond   its bearing was beside us   and direct on top
and the other side   which had us pinned down hemmed in   and it was lazy
the way planets are   whose orbits have settled now   without cause to change
without cause to change   and lacking even one eye   came on us blindly

like apostrophes   not the punctuation marks   the figure of speech
an address to things   enabling their attendance   imaginably
if implausibly   not that that's much of a test   O Hurricane Wind!
O Solar Raystorm!   O Serendipitous Breeze!   O Harsh Northern Wind!
they called it a beast   they called it Leviathan   its legs were orange
it grew horns and tail   it bellowed and flames came forth   it chased us around
we grew our own shells   called them churches and chapels   I had forgotten

once again green fields   once again the dogs barking   once again the news
no strike on airlines   the jobs no one ever leaves   how the yen and mark
old watering parts   a kind of pressure fitting   a cracked pistol spray
bamboo garden stakes   the room's home-made wiring chart   a can of mixed screws
a tin-covered chest   warping sheets of masonite   rust on the steel parts

I keep forgetting

I keep forgetting   it was a gray-greenish strand   on the boulevard
a flimsy cabin   a spider or butterfly   I heard it or saw
swagged in the cypress   learning to draw fish or whales   at our Sunday School
with a sliding door   a hydraulic lift device   and I was helpless
I was alone then   and it was tangled with vines   they were deciding

it seems like they did   gave me some food to help out   face pretty mushed up
that was the next year   the year dominos counted   and Chinese checkers
there was still a tree   then burning grass, someone's pool   the brown thrasher then
plaster of paris   footprints of raccoons or dogs   the pond and its park
I walked over there   a basement barbershop there   sometimes a drugstore
magazines about rape   stories about why no one   was willing to help
I keep forgetting   I think it was on Central   maybe Hydraulic

or by the Price house   those huge shade trees and brick streets   heavy bicycle
had to learn my way   withstood a love big as that   hanging out downtown
when it was so hot   eating egg foo young they sold   stools, a countertop
could take a bus there   cherished air conditioning   their own trampoline
no one got injured   did we take our glasses off   did we flip over

Quarreling at night

quarreling at night   like they'd been caged together   weren't sure they liked it
might make this the end   or at least lay down the rules   no stroking unless
compromise wedges   little ones left all over   like a mine field here
you can't mention it   it's hostile to throw them out   you guys need a truce
or some other war   distractions a hairdresser   a trip to Europe

acquired bad habits   got attached to the wrong stuff   sitting there watching
indifferent to   pick at some more rotten flesh   nothing's repulsive
everything is   crumbled old letters away   destroyed evidence
waited to dissolve   never quite getting that far   wake and it's morning
wake and it's morning   sleep through work as best you can   slog through lists of lists
a world of needs still   dissolving doesn't happen   sharper-edged maybe
poking flabby you   you snap back, stun them briefly   they return with knives

who lives by, dies by   it would be nicer to die   you start up one day
they slap you for that   time to keep things to yourself   you thought you did though
you say you'll go walk   a suitable day for it   you head for water
famous people jumped   famous people walked in slow   fame no help to them
their one solution   it was what they could think of   couldn't help or stop

Taking the night train

taking the night train   in the rattle there rattle   the steel the keen keen
bound the valley through   dark tunnel dreamtunneling   snow streaming onto
the slick the quicktrip   throughout the whole bone heatnight   juice in the morning
tickets and your pass   don't forget your ▮ belonging   you checked off and bounced
jingling in the glass   flicks of lights the cities twitch   rattle in a dream

meant drifting weed seed   among modern asepsis   technical ▮ questions
opened iris-like   camera shutter machine   a room with an egg
boiled in a far land   sucked on a wooden splinter   carried a mountain
a calf down the hill   a starry cart responded   the rocks he sat on
compass in his hand   heroic figure of ▮ bad   would be Blake's Newton
you've been awarded   two decades of crossword subs   there they go buying
logs rolled from rivers   the boys survived who were hurt   thrilled till they were killed

▮ waking alone moaning   stand in a darkened chamber   swinging pipes around
a little drummer   for her fourth birthday round-up   got a western dress
residual phlegm   kept waking shaken and back   hit a long tunnel
hit a quiet lake   mist rising in cold morning   a fish ripples it
moose tracks in the mud   they had their showdown right here   it ▮ would have been *awe*

Rototillering

rototillering   within the thin skin of dirt   not quite the cone's whorl
not one simple whorl   multiple branchings of it   enlarging sizes
quickly uneven   quickly uneven-seeming   uneven-seeming
bending to converse   a frail old woman sitting   on a patio
behind a railing   on the sunny quiet side   the garden's out back

marked the officials   barriers like big root-arms   big fenceposts big trees
and steered clear therefrom   also the little shoe store   which was her pleasure
where seasons always   fashions and fashion's factions   nice your dropping by
getting around things   not evading the *BIG* things   finding a firm path
never enough cloaks   if you're speaking of my faults   that's circumvented
the crusty swirled in   the tender sandy brought up   it's cooked we're ready
you can release me   there was delicate thunder   wetter getting worse

too melancholy   appeals to some not   a son on the staff
sunlight on the staff   sun on the musical staff   a son dragged his staff
there was spare polish   always lots more work to do   between the corn rows
frightening root-knobs   entangled in the cane break   sloughed-off as echoes
lugged back to the house   not that we'll eat so many   just to be more safe

Filling the dump truck

filling the dump truck   a small white lawn-care size one   with mowed-up tree-fall
broad coal-shovelfuls   from piles the boss keeps forming   raking the yard clean
someone's below me   removing shutters I guess   we share our insects
a house fly right now   I get to hear their banter   see flowers trampled
this work MUST BE DONE   if the results imagined   to be brought about

that' s reassuring   otherwise you might just quit   doing what you're told
being paid less sucks   but if the work is honest   and there's no other
tire tracks curving out   I'm becoming dents in grass   formed from the moisture
and the honest weight   certified by agencies   powerful machines
old people walk left   return walking right / come back   strange channel for news
problem with the feed   bounced down in from Canada   migrating I guess
big flocks of duck duck   responded with little naps   a sense of New York

my little dearie   founded-a-dynasty one   couldn't *help* being
more flowers for springs   felt an exotic hunger   resented zero
hammer develops   crept snakelike because hunting   tissue teaparty
what present to buy   glasses if they can't read signs   built himself triumphs
built follies for her   someone has to take charge now   not the blackbirds please

FIFTEEN

Backward unzipping

backward unzipping   including its rephrasing   at higher volumes
beside denial   setting that apart no fear   climbed in in reverse
trying to unskin   carefully rubbed fold by fold   (frisbee flew to hand)
(they went practicing)   or wrestling feather shadows   (held a good long loft)
by then the phone rang   the *ZACHAROPLASTEION*   our table's ready

brought three exemplars   the smallest one still seems shield   one's an act of prayer
caught in the open   the largest's degenerate   spent itself wildly
I got a postcard   with an Ipousteguy guy   *Man Pushing the Door*
I was pushing one   it no longer had a jamb   it lay in the woods
surrounded by cones   more cones than animals eat   could have been a trick
below the door, what?   entrance to the jewel room?   hide-out for robbers?
nothing under it   yellowed ferns, dry pine needles   hunched down to study

kicked up a ruckus   grew tailfeathers and hopped in   started Friday noon
arbitrary greens   loose seasonal packaging   no more Wintergreen
he pushed here here here   is caught there and there and there   expanded torso
organic enmeshed   in his own inorganic   not a silence HERE
nor silence BEFORE   definitely not *haiku*   because I said so

Why don't we just quit

why don't we just quit   why don't we drop kick from here   Old Hickory says
we could bend under   no secrets the plot turns on   to get to Old Yes
among the rare reefs   those weird yellow pouch-back fish   it meant snorkeling
so what's beyond that   found an empty bottle there   during the mowing
playing hooky here   stopped explaining or trying   the limp fish of it

motor sprang to life   hack cough jeez uhwak uhwak   graphic purity
the next corner club   settled spurious trembles   really you made me
tenderly trembled   *brave vibration each way free*   liked a new necklace
went past a horsecart   went past and did double takes   broke the coconut
forgotten something   I knew it was wrong but still   whose parents yelled at
then when the trucks came   usually nicer there   delicate elm shade
then the seeds piled up   then the little leaves falling   sweet smoke of leaf piles

Columbus said no   Hernando de Soto no   Cadillac La Salle
no turning back now   but always backward-turning   finding beginnings
seeking departures   resembling innovations   nothing changes but
I can't feel the same   not a novel about you   simple thing of cat
attacking stray ties   the little plastic wire things   from the grocery

Sounded like theory

sounded like theory   quarreled and quibbled like it   felt like kids again
videotalkers   never need to be pimples   felt chidden again
blue caterpillar   the empire of Genghiz Khan   amazed by music
unnerved her a bit   it shouldn't have been so blue   but it meant something
modal/modular   disgorged a large study group   white yes blue haired ones

in the doubt of rage   could just punch a zero in   an insipid taste
by all means and fat   verdigris had a magic   resembling punish
which is hypnosis   the state of finding new things   have to climb fences
I'm not thinking that   though I appreciate you   are scarred and sacred
wants to be native   without fetching the water   wants to be well fed
can't stop this peeking   into people's private planes   everything is
scared of wanting so   to be emboldened by it   my little apple

they knocked on my door   they wanted me to do things   which they then gave me
a calmer weather   though the wind was glistening   tore the drops off it
what is the next-best   being a basic black gown   being plaid suspenders
protesting her love   proud of what she does to men   won't surrender now
made papier-mâché   considered a basket lunch   cut the personnel

Just argued to win

just argued to win   said what made sense at that point   then said what fell next
shaped his thought that way   thought it was dialectics   and he had a goal
world, don't exclude me   the bananas never cared   the silverware yawned
no that was Disney   the silverware *continued*   there *were* rebel yawns
there was assembled   at that time a good posse   which set out at night

extra long lace wings   the white gloves of prettiness   disjointed, sadly
with her disturbed man   her thunderous corseting   her ravaged troopship
thinking like a queen   you have to start royally   someone was the first
really crazy then   but force would be a helpful   bowing to the good
you'd have some henchmen   rebel band of friends from school   or from down the shop
or your chess buddies   hey that would be a cool one   story based on chess
how would the knight move   understood as storyline   two squares and sideways

thought it a redbird   lowered antennae again   *why not let it out?*
if there was pity   dim and out of the background   and he had to twist
something's different   I wasn't looking and now   they can laugh at them
their prerogative   their grotto and eyrie right   their romantic souls
the angles altered   when you see from your sofa   she's offering but

I guess you're okay

I guess you're okay   proportionately honored   tender on record
trusted by minims   charged with the care of hearses   it should read *horses*
it should read *thyrsus*   I'm new at these classicals   Caesar recitals
what my friend calls them   gets syncopated again   terrible train wreck
frankly drank a lot   ever thereafter took pills   keeping a life raft

but on the car roof   against God's mean punishment   so much rain IS mean
but there was one such   a flood and probably sex   gone sodomistic
it's not meant for that   pleasure nor can the mind be   both on the same stalk
right there in Eden   well before Oprah baby   I don't want to know
you're still looking good   that is I mean I guess so   not granite but but
had his boat becalmed   didn't think it was his fault   shows what he had learned
a hell of a lot   learned as a balloon learns air   pressing into it

she'll have to inquire   because our plans have changed so   in a sort of way
too hard to explain   oh dear we had inquiries   wrote to a panel
pictures in the news   became a Green candidate   wrote from misery
from a *lucky* joy   chairs were bolted, *luckily*   nothing of us was
his slave mistress felt   she had learned to be refined   she emptied the trash

Maybe you're no fraud

maybe you're no fraud   if you can't prostitute that   no science to say
you can hit potholes   you can feel bodily warmth   as a free given
jumping through the door   roll the skin up first then jump   teaching skydiving
moderate freezes   it's just hard to say it right   little grass runway
a calm black shepherd   worn-out muddy stretch of road   wearing just sheer hose

a leather jacket   bending like a diver there   speaking to a john
that was the paper   fluttered in as compulsive   mixing a swirl cake
easier to prey   on who is asking for it   in a high-cut thong
it could figure then   like the weather foggy first   then turning cooler
green Russian warplane   a white Cessna two-seater   garbagemen talking
another lame one   limping and spitting her drool   little cobblestones
remarked on hunger   the problem directing it   not so generous

it was the airstream   she generally felt well   she looked terrific
if you weren't hung up   can't help but express express   still kept his pants on
doubt anyone cares   the great primary colors   a blue sign outside
blue on a white wing   they left me here but watched me   the whole nastiness
she pulled it open   she drifted rushing the daze   came to a landing

Doing a great job

doing a great job   fighting the freeze blowing in   from the hole way off
lousy tunnel end   it's like refrigeration   outside compression
the press of finish   blowing into a large space   suddenly cooler
feels directionless   tough to move around or see   the Lucifer dream
as Dante saw him   zapped frozen in place in pride   desires still engraved

as you have known them   as crustaceans present them   as the ice keeps them
and a shriek knows them   as wandering Apache   as no one wants jobs
and they don't have them   as a helicopter base   from a war now done
as you can shield it   among sell-outs industries   chants of the long ride
into frozen lands   into uttermost bizarre   as the silent stall
the shuttered market   lines of greed and grief carved in   as the blade's keeper
the blade's sharpener   as the guillotine must fall   they don't clean the block

that would be tidy   silly to be so tidy   it's just a building
scarce materials   no ample materials   so much so scattered
scree down the mountain   many small rocks many large   from icy regions
in a pride of work   scraping, with a weepy eye   and an African
asked me if I were   and I had to say all are   all are but he left

Redundant dancers

redundant dancers   rejected muscles and skin   but carved nonetheless
a kind of aphid   a kind of aphid-eater   eaters of that kind
making a long dance   their concert got great reviews   there were some who cried
it was spectacle   story of the brave defense   and the fall of Troy
recalled by Rob Roy   enacted in the dreams of   Catherine the Great

William Tell dances   holding his hungry crossbow   a giant comes in
juggles like Atlas   you'll never go home again   and it ends with love
our simple desire   to fulfill our body's task   over and over
the stage has babies   that's the final scene, babies   about a thousand
just wearing diapers   most of them cold and bawling   some hungry or sick
some calm ones sleeping   and the two or three alert   Buddha-eyed aware
but you can't find them   the ones you might really need   but you know they're there

then the curtain falls   there are giants depicted   they look like headsmen
it's not the first scene   the friendly billows of clouds   above active seas
there's a slow panic   we stumble off through the park   homeless men shouting
there's a barrel fire   I'm stuck in rocks on a hill   too dark to go down
something touches me   at the corner of my lip   it is warm and wet

Sitting here thinking

sitting here thinking   a process *going forward*   that's what *process* means
but it's not like that   no it's like that but it's not   I sense a sequence
the birds doing it   they weren't doing that last week   an array exists
an unrollingness   or a being-drawn-toward-ness   a large sucking thing
making us happen   not so much as a goal might   but just to get *there*

though it's more *then* then   not so much a state or place   and not elected
though if it's a wave   one can surf along, or bob   waiting for one's call
never learning *stand*   or *fall* never *wiping out*   not that that's crazy
just a bit lonely   *where* was I or *when* was I?   discoursing gaily
of the furry flux   whose moment can't be simple   hence the fur image
levels of texture   including the worn patches   down to bare red raw
though not of course *down*   *among* more the idea   among this flux-wealth

she will think her plan   you will head off for England   he is testing drugs
Joyce thinks and thinks Joyce   I'm watching the blebby lights   dancing on my eyes
we have stolen fire   we have told ourselves a lie   we want to converse
no we don't that's wrong   we've erected languages   to keep us talking
we can't distinguish   no we can that's just *the* thing   we can distinguish

They had to receive

they had to receive   couldn't just encrust others   they'd had to moult off
they'd had to finance   now they had to be financed   and stuff to swallow
one replaced the bulbs   timbers splintered in the wind   it was quite sudden
there was no warning   there was a white handkerchief   signified a man
there was some lightning   we'd had the new rod installed   no one was worried

ceremonies trailed   serially connected   when the bonfire blazed
no it was sudden   of whichever thing you saw   these paltry results
among multitudes   excused him because of it   permitted her child
permitted her dog   they had to be bundled up   off by parcel post
we had the railways   we had natural bounty   amid acid rain
that surfboard's quirky   disguised or blinded to it   caught napping again
had to pay this time   the piper came up whining   beneath our station

another station   investigated such things   parallel life forms
talking aliens   imagined new Olympics   who cries the largest
kvetched the whole long way   as if there's nothing to do   or no place to go
there was ripping out   and slapping it onto you   there was no chance now
we were three weeks late   postcards of bunnies kissing   all the wrong colors

It was easy then

it was easy then   when no one was having fun   to paint great pictures
our degraded time   goes by flashing good humor   or just plain flashing
what do good minds do   twiddle with computer code   or package to sell
or get up on stage   with a magic rhythm band   and do say sing act
some design buildings   some will get built but not all   some hit the scrap heap

where no one's laughing   on account of the hunger   then there's the anger
these must be great times   for painting masterpieces   you know what that means
for transposing dreams   into images or cash   hired handsome lawyers
whose firm goes bankrupt   shared the business cycle   shared the fitness club
as an example   interviewed a designer   on a Ferris wheel
resisted and fled   left things a mess for her team   drew dew from the clouds
bevies of beauties   advertising auto sex   kids in the exhaust

there's a line between   rage and remembering rage   well since they called him
they've crossed over it   the rest of us will suffer   that won't be new here
you can hear marching   before you see it swarming   that's a film device
you saw a great film   what was it called can you say   with old war symbols
sex and love's fine line   staying up past dawn unquenched   still willing to hope

It's pointing at me

it's pointing at me   as a child of certainty   of catastrophe
its name is holy   I call it guilt but that's wrong   just because it is
not because it's not   but the holy part is tough   rubber on a pipe
which makes a weapon   kind or quiet or easy   easier to use
more mistakable   I'm excited by pliant   and by pliancy

a sinister point   a region beyond aching   first erasure then
oblivion then   nothing ever is the same   we might make new friends
I'm going to bed   I'm going to meet the dead   I do it often
last night I met Strauss   I thought him the musician   he was a stand-in
night before, Disney   before that I met women   Florence Nightingale
she complained a lot   all good nurses do, they say   but Mary Shelley
you wouldn't believe   remarkably hot sexpot   that's the word she used

there were some dead slaves   they came all at once one night   not one of them talked
my great great granddad   he came one time, showed his wound   he seemed to hold back
he might have spoken   but his horse spooked and he went   and one nasty night
crazier than these   Toussaint-Louverture himself   wore a tricorner
he spoke; he said *March!*   I saw the wall's edge coming   there was no stopping

Juice is where it starts

juice is where it starts   so=much=for=breakfast=then=lunch   the cycle of food
then — the sky — TA DA!   we've ALREADY met the stars   joked about the rest
we yawn back dully   hate excites my emotions   not just hate alone
not just emotions   also cruelty — *all acts   RUN by emotion*
which is about all   our behavior amounts to   please have her call me

which had root flavor   soon as I picked it I knew   it had a good chance
it was like garlic   it could be easily boxed   ruin come slowly
got married right there   the lodge on Shelter Island   glad to help with clams
decked (decorated)   *decked* meaning *knocked to the floor*   or having the floors
such oilinesses   never without her knowing   descent into ooze
in a metal vat   blades pressing through and harder   pressing out the oil
as they have to do   industry is industry   his not a bad lot

we could use more hints   even the fish aren't explained   that's the movie's fault
couldn't pull the plug   had it in my hand but quaked   meant to put socks on
they always eat schmaltz   excused to enter the church   was working late there
she'd had enough men   but was still married alas   she turned to magic
it got done with tools   can you guess what I'm thinking   too bad — you'd go far

Like tourists we stopped

like tourists we stopped   having seen in the greenhouse   their surprising forms
perfectly normal   all but the quiet farm road   the northern climate
everything wrong   contextually speaking   to find ostriches
a breeding couple   raised for their eggs or their meat   not enough room though
cooped in a glass house   the whole long dark winter doom   specks on the Earth's skin

still we were chased off   angry farmer and his dog   guess he's being sued
can't take a picture   can't make a ballad from it   have to talk of larks
climbing from the fields   swinging back down to silence   silence in the grass
sun, splendid breezes   always vanishing musics   another trash bag
roadside litterings   as an inhabited land   with avant-garde sounds
coming from far off   speaking an extreme wisdom   felt as hedonists
the day began well   then it exploded warnings   who abandoned us

who would have hired scabs   who made an expedition   entrusting sherpas
hired coolies and serfs   hired Grub Street Tin Pan Alley   went by in landaus
back and forth with gloves   sweet skins touched only by silk   treasured like giltwork
children raised to play   no one raised to hard labor   production questions
a Sargasso Sea   salted, buttered the popcorn   there's just time to watch

Tried to brush them off

tried to brush them off   light specks in the dark photo   crocus on the grass
in the wide shade band   above which two ear shadows   not ears but from trees
not trees with leaves yet   underwater coral fans   branching like nerve nets
onto the lit band   of grass in morning sunlight   that was days ago
now the twigs are thick   the shadows denser, ball-like   a gift when he comes

here, here, now go play   I must be alone with her   there's a leafing out
private transactions   not like gangsters terrorists   tender aging touch
scars and liver spots   hands that have thatched roofs moved rocks   have built and broken
peeled fruit and ironed   written letters in the night   unsure what results
letters that mattered   in the struggle between wills   owning and loving
getting and giving   hands that are so familiar   they will not fly off
though they flutter here   like birds in the leafing trees   speaking and seeking

grateful for summer   basking in her leg's warmth then   in her back's slow curve
taking again her nipple   kissing its quick reflex rise   hand on her belly
so many children made   out making new involvements   new hands on new skin
fingers and lips so   our sexes touch making touch   making lovemaking
this delight blinds me   the slide into you around   tangling limbs and sheets

Highlighted the news

highlighted the news   minutely local items   slightly undercut
price-war victory   unadulterated war   each unit each year
found a bank of sleep   as welcome as night to birds   as dawn to hunter
and to homeless men   or a job to the jobless   who stand now and count
watching others work   missing the feel of floured skin   living with a smell

who was a blacksmith   ornamental ironwork   and a ferrier
and had other lives   a museum of new art   wearing memory
as a dress-up gown   always anticipating   tender and timid
riddles abounding   it being almost Sunday   left an open gate
arriving too late   concerted tractor solo   Communist ethic
the audience coughed   had to get out quick and breathe   seems modern enough
open as we go   stumbled on a jewel cache   this changes enough

might it not change you   to have ventured and then won   their hospital show
showing such ventures   so you rub against the goods   days without chain saws
months without gunshots   looks just like his father did   back when we were kids
divided the reeds   looked through his binoculars   yes it's a beaver
he swats the water   disappeared as a stage trick   had already gone

She saw this in Rome:

she saw this in Rome: one threw his shutters open   to use a cell phone
which is like writing —   speaking into atmosphere —   not quite without walls
get a clear angle   up to satellites and stars   with the best tools yet
make the big gesture   leave those below wonderment   even jealousy
to whom does it go   *which of us is getting it*   he's also yelling

we can all hear it   often swallowed by traffic   that's what she found there
Shelley rewritten   the non-virtual skylarks   singing as they climb
an ascending song   subsiding into silence   returning to grass
this reassures me   since art can't be eternal   can't come from the stars
the idea of   revelation's attractive   if we're in control
and we get to talk   but it's weird from the outside   for the working stiff
or even for me   who works to make the ends meet   still gets to have fun

sticking kind of close   to the drift-shifting moment   not holding the line
holding many lines   often very short small strands   and setting them down
one then another   here's one on biking on sand   kind of touch and go
once in Portugal   drank his 50-year-old wine   saved by his father
for his son's pleasure   now there's a ceremony   oh he loved us so

SIXTEEN

Monster hog (black/chrome)

monster hog (black/chrome)   made me blank out a second   being bought and sold
where I stopped to ask   directions for the bike route   off into the woods
inside someone knew   I was already on it   curled me back around
into sandy trails   mushrooms under the beech trees   just not yet ready
don't suggest falling   on the protuberances   much too familiar

blank out repeated   not finding there a self-myth   instead instructions
muffled charter boat   a sign from the deeps (way down)   a different life
caught between glass plates   held in a hard killing light   looked at through a tube
crisped another time   heading for a museum   it's that big thing dream
canted till it came   wanted to give it a name   resolved to forget
ended up walking   got to the edge of Utah   they felt the earthquake
back in Reykjavik   back in Anchorage beat down   like the thumb of God

they had boards laid out   climbing up the loose cinders   the recent blow-top
of Mt. St. Helens   forest laid out as splinters   a catastrophe
found recovery   some of the victims preserved   the Pompeii process
mastered by evil   figured in some comic books   slipped into the flux
welcomed at the door   too late to back out from here   has a deathly grip

Nine pay telescopes

nine pay telescopes   overlooking sheer distance   children keep running
back to Momma's purse   five more minutes of scanning   the ocean for whales
what's not to enjoy   watching the little ones grow   stronger, more eager
worth stacks of quarters   also buying time to read   the news, drink coffee
participate in   the world's sexy give-and-take   life on the boardwalk

juxtapose that with   this other family, *his*,   whose kids dare not ask
but stand in shadows   yearning from behind a line   and time has run out
they slip in the car   glide away without impact   without mementos
or *their* strategy   bring their own binoculars   go out on the boat
take the guided tours   sample the local giftshops   buy fun things for friends
avoid saying no   without always saying yes   don't ask why this is
don't recite Tolstoy   accept one as not so wrong   one as not so right

the waves keep breaking   gulls police the work of crabs   in part timelessly
not like they once thought   more contingent and precious   specific and rare
each unique event   magnified from small causes   hence this broad diction
with its own fictions   completely unbuyable   the pay telescopes
long malfunctioning   replaced by aquaria   making a profit

Did a cossack dance

did a cossack dance   allemande left, do-si-do   slipped on the rumba
for a home movie   where it will seem sci-fi strange   requiring big words
they're spreading manure   they brought hearing devices   they danced with tables
held them in their teeth   always turning in the wind   stopping to listen
a few steps deeper   let me be kissed by the fog   as the flowers wilt

might as well let go   let the tugged glider drift off   brand-new flowers now
what about *brand-new*   all these slim bodies hormones   you can laugh at it
their TV sex scenes   which is anti-commandment   taking *x* in vain
not *SILENT SIDEWALKS*   we're reaching into others   clothes and privacies
checking their faces   what are the signs of distress   that you've *gone too far*
had to do it in   three minutes or in scare-quotes   it's your decision
I've found a fresh birth   between the pine tree gullies   in the lifting wind

controlling the drag   what else is there to master   we've done the take-off
we've done the landing   long as we avoid weather   I can look at him
I like how his eyes   it's not a thing to fight off   it sounds clearer now
I love my strong fears   I am as naked as that   I am climbing now
reaching the last point   when we'll let the cable slip   we go into light

Lake Baikal has seals

Lake Baikal has seals   Earth's only freshwater seals   (local news item)
let's see what that means   first of all how'd they get there   — swam up a river
maybe five hundred   thousand years ago and changed   along the journey
probably fishing   when the fish were migrating   up their fish ladders
or stopped in stages   planting colonies upstream   which then disappeared

what seems strange and rare   grew somehow from something plain   is then the moral
and replicates things   we readily understand   which is exciting
which is wonderful   which means there's room for wonder   it's not just for kids
some things are for kids   like being swung in circles   but leaf boats are neat
if you find a brook   and nutshell boats are better   stick a mast in mud
stick a leaf sail on   watch as they go drifting down   bobbing and tipping
oops mine's gone under   yours is still bumping along   uh oh an eddy

one acts like baby   sister pushes the stroller   then they trade it's hard
this could be called love   it could be called role-playing   or just regression
or it's scratch-my-back-   and-I'll-scratch-yours, which is good   if you play your part
how can I make you   as happy as you deserve   if I just screw you
or make you pregnant   and go on to another   noticing nothing

Heard a bunch of Bach

heard a bunch of Bach   not fiddles an old organ   Sunday in the park
allowed to travel   to crawl off the leash a bit   instead of fearing
out loud unravelled   they changed the plans it's raining   not a friendly door
where's the pleasure now   in just a bunch of ball play   a team leaving us
finding a new spot   they'll still understand Bach there   no point in sorrow

spun the honey pot   learned about a special way   hated thinking so
who'll be your friend now   going to welcome the drone   how blues comes across
by the large extreme   am the happiest person   able to ignore
sitting by the ditch   chucking stones in the water   lopping off the weeds
switch with the hot wind   pull the legs off grasshoppers   squirt them with fluid
sizzled on the walk   tiny tortures from grade school   (he said they'd seen it)
I'm sorry we're closed   there's too much misery loose   genetic functions

seldom such bad news   giving swastika tattoos   each to the other
blend quail and chicken   guess you get a smart chicken   a quail brain who thinks
how did I get here   they gave me the wrong body   refuses to cluck
the woods are leaving   no habitat to hide in   all my thoughts in words
enough to warn you   had a magnificent time   we've suffered damage

Banged away at it

banged away at it   aimed to distract and sneak in   certainly might work
theory drivel   got a big pile and shoveled   that's the cheesy stink
announced her presence   big low-cut and boobs held up   slinking here to there
can't deny bounty   real soil he bends down to kiss   now who goosed that man
always played the fool   just couldn't think normally   everyone knew

when they were alone   there was a tricky séance   one of the previews
the spirits jingled   mainly garbage but whose fault   a few nuggets left
ROSES THERE FOR YOU   no one claimed to know a thing   unfortunately
or fortunately   no guide for the seduction   GREEN EYES GOOD PLANNING
a toy tax shelter   usual scuz in the bath   back deck steps crumbling
pool floor clean but rough   over the fence for a stroll   these floods keep coming
no more theater   keeping things about the same   grandparents aging

whirled on the freeway   drove into some pretty spots   sea lions sunning
a mission from God   so funny and based on guilt   the next time around
he likes old Hitchcocks   they both like old Errol Flynns   who likes the Reagans
Bedtime for Bonzo   shouldn't make it easier   for the rich or else
we'll all just wither   wither or get like Withers   don't choose Dagwood's boss

Well it goes backwards

well it goes backwards   expresses relentlessly   mixed bits of nature
the blue rain of trees   crystal forests where birds sing   lullaby true north
embodied visions   just as if the world mattered   only as symbol
put it behind you   freshening accentuate   can't wait to cut free
bound by virtuals   all right it's a tornado   that's too convenient

watched a show on porn   got to pretend it wasn't   the stage audience
the land of cable   invested in her spike heels   the background candles
sweet culture critic   about to break his table   the urge to harangue
the pheasant's brain genes   slipped into a chicken's code   you already know
it's really just news   not like Greek independence   now there's a subject
not that it's not one   but it mattered more back when   1820 say
what they really need   is Greek independence now   we all need that now

we need the great goods   it's the selfishness goes wrong   so why are we so
it's not tree magic   do you like being barked at   figuratively
that is by people   no which is why moth magnets   I don't trust iron
that suicide cage   over Nevada Falls' lip   the man who set it
had a harness on   you're invited to stand there   that's much much too much

She's too flirtatious

she's too flirtatious   she goes after the flowers   rubbing their anthers
but he was waiting   his video camera   caught them coming out
its head slipped and drooped   oops now it's shooting the floor   a slow fall at first
between snow and sand   defined the temperate One   song drifts from their church
then there was justice   who bruises the oranges   who crumples the plan

staging our next play   involved with the producer   fit into his wound
enabled free time   restraining worried mothers   kept the grounds guarded
one by one the ducks   shot with the pretend rifle   then they popped back up
it was carnival   the guy took his clothes with him   threw them in the lake
through this tiny hole   in an invisible slit   microscopic sperm
that was a line-up   they sometimes get the right guy   it can go both ways
got to try it once   controlling the two motors   into the wave line

when they summarized   it stood out completely fresh   the One who wasn't
the clock was friendly   only because he forgot   the fewer choices
a bundle of grass   it would replace the old thatch   for the doll's teahouse
as such a father   retired from the industry   circling the tower
hello line of cars   line of drivers arguing   running out of gas

Having found the notes

having found the notes   tied them in melody strings   dispersed them neatly
then to screw around   that's when it starts starts starts to   grew interesting
little things with wings   wings with some kind of feathers   the size of a crow
had to be preying   already they were insects   from eons ago
other lizard things   that niches are relaxes: EACH one is FED on

a male lap dancer   come to sit on you sweetheart   look at this it's yours
not now but later   of course that will really cost   more than what you've paid
but I'm a hunk's hunk   I never have problems there   doesn't matter who
shadow, reflection   yes he'd better know this now   it won't change a thing
field mouse is happy   whispering through the fieldcorn   that still goes along
also he's naked   cute little pink paws and nose   thin coat of short fur
rubbed against my foot   totally captivated   then started running

lost track of glasses   suppose the surgery failed   what else could deter
who cried for three days   whose life was reconfigured   who was crucified
just as a small thief   still had to lug his own cross   look I don't WANT to
like dig your own grave   write your own funeral dirge   deliver a speech
taped one for later   dearly belovéd thank you   its sad beginning

Still life in old dump

still life in old dump   tapestry with city scene   tiles from a shower
mostly grass-covered   the warning sign knocked down though   and broken in two
Schut /und Asche /ver   on one side of the road, *te   /abladen /boten*
on the other side   (don't dump debris and ashes)   *looks* like a landfill
an old bike way off   in a hollow no two bikes   and a tricycle

please don't do that please   reporting on what you've done   cataloging slides
here you're trying hard   to be so cool and then poof   you go and blow it
it's bad enough with   admitting intuition   and not dressing right
your bad music taste   your liking Hollywood corn   it goes on they're right
there's a way to push   self out of writing and keep   writing meaningful
like the side-by-side   display of dictionaries   East and West German
back before the change   the Webster's equivalent   under the word *selbst*

or SELF a column   in the Communist version   two in the Western
West is more selfish   the point precisely detailed   no intuition
an idea yes   shown with formal harmony   verbal-visual
what can you call it   who says you have to name it   I'd like to honor
Uwe Warnke here   whose little work I've described   plagiarized maybe

Maps you'd like as friends

maps you'd like as friends   what if that doesn't work out   pick a direction
then a dimension   you take derision lightly   not a healthy plan
if division comes   ooh that sounds like it could hurt   they've feared defection
increased detection   collected his reflections   with his connections
seems like a kid's game   they benefit from our doubt   it's delusory

we play dealer's choice   mainly stud poker and draw   set a bet-limit
reduces bluffing   too bad in a way but fair   people get greedy
not that we're worried   because of our *Biberbau*   the truth's coming out
keep winking it off   too many German signposts   that was the last one
at least for a while   I have to agree Tokyo   Tokyo Singapore
it was a short talk   didn't understand a thing   let's go be hippies
the corpus corpus   always ate the little kids   mostly for Easter

we were invited   then we were disinvited   then re-invited
they invented why   we smiled and went to watch them   we broke a tooth off
we went rolling home   something followed us back here   couldn't throw it out
or toss it candy   well we could, we did, now what   it's licking ankles
the paper was blunt   I'm dreaming of tall hats now   fancy mini-cars

OK I'll do it

OK I'll do it   stay late so you'll beat me up   skip food for a week
fall off the I-beam   jump not knowing how to swim   lie in the oven
I consent to it   if that will make you happy   cut my stomach out
pull my joints apart   cut my tongue out and slice me   use me how you will
stick objects in me   dement me with crazy drugs   make me a robot

torture my children   make me look at what you do   use me to shit on
recite love poems   while you pull out nails and hair   go at me with tools
tiny power sanders   electric drills staple guns   flay me like a roast
feed me my own flesh   treat me so it hurts longer   gouge my eyes half out
wrap me in shaved ice   put me in a box with snakes   show me my tendons
make me hang by thumbs   have me crawl across hot coals   press nails in my ears
let me heal a while   teach me to make poison gas   to make explosives

have me build huge bombs   make me strangle newborn babes   jab knives in people
then jab me some more   give me horrible cancer   let me dwindle down
bring me back again   give it to me once again   again and again
praise me for living   make me burn down hospitals   poison the rivers
make autos explode   make me teach others your hate   make me keep watching

In one there were wolves

in one there were wolves   you turned a light out and ran   barely reached the stairs
one had low ceilings   in parts a cave-like dirt floor   a wringer washer
one was filled with cans   you couldn't stand up in it   and ammo boxes
one had his dad's saw   a retrofitted bathroom   a guest room or den
one's got an old fridge   a place for the cats to hide   new ping-pong set-up

one's got a garage   with a Lexus inside it   and a PC room
a coal bin in one   a huge coal furnace to stoke   maybe nothing else
another had pipes   they were all wrapped with hot tape   you had to plug in
one had barn siding   a desk and library shelves   also a work bench
a sewing room there   closets trunks and a dummy   broken light fixtures
one was much too moist   mold grew on everything   ruined sci-fi books
he had ten fish tanks   in his or maybe fourteen   that gave him some peace

one had a print shop   drawers of type, letterpress   and a multilith
in one they taught dance   how to rock around the clock   back in the Fifties
in one they talked wild   anarchy and hypnotism   a man named Schwartzbart
in one a wood shop   where he made coffee table   and dining table
one a water bed   someone else's lovemaking   a kind of envy

The sounds of passage

the sounds of passage   moving in ways that cross mine   jets sometimes close by
hard heels on sidewalk   the stray fly which found my head   I fidget and scratch
the chair and fabric   dogs and music not far off   the air I inhale
then slowly exhale   probability suggests   some were molecules
Cicero inhaled   the nitrous matter unchanged   pushed clean through his lungs

part of his noises   in his time before airplanes   his wagon clatter
hammers and chisels   the oxen lowing so loud   and always a wind
or birds hard at it   making their space to live in   their own song cages
not to go alone   into nothingness silence   or be left a stone
a hillside with goats   thus to be stepped on stood on   clicked into the stream
its own small babble   or when the hard rain sheets down   and the mud hill shifts
drifting to the sea   broadening alluvia   elsewhere islands rise

tractors keep going   there seems to be a pattern   surrounding sound walls
he had just learned how   hearing the digitized calm   environment-noise
when a new version   making people unhappy   left something back there
guess we'll have to leave   leave it behind do without   sound of thoughts out loud
inside the brain space   and slippery translations   wants to trade tickets

Stepped on the flowers

stepped on the flowers   because it was his nature   and his paragraph
then it was her turn   she made real model airplanes   flew them in the park
the ones with motors   tiny Cessnas and Beechcrafts   then the page ended
a new paragraph   involved a couple talking   at first they were calm
then they disagreed   it was a fight about space   time or attention

we never learned what   and the next paragraph swept   off to the distance
with a funny man   who seemed to adore people   but spent three months off
in remote mountains   playing keyboards and writing   collage consommés
also milking goats   and making cheese like Heidi's   strong old grandpapa
another page-end   new page, new paragraph, new   female character
whose first paragraph   seems to be nothing but tears   she has a disease
affecting her eyes   so her weeping's bodily   not from the spirit

her next paragraph   how she used to hate women   hated being one
you know that story   her final paragraph though   a funny hotel
with a fountain court   trout in the pool and parrots   guests got parasols
the birds flew around   the most friendly came so close   they nibbled your ears
you could feed them seeds   two of them talked: he'd say *So*   she'd say *Whatchuwant*

This is pretty if

this is pretty if   alders ringing the marshland   lying on some grass
birds hopping like springs   it might have been better but   their songs crazier
a baseball event   there's not always but these days   comet in the night
hung up her laundry   laughed about the place he lived   went off on their bikes
whittling by the fax   got your machine am sorry   signed without feeling

because the ripple   there have to be frogs and snakes   because explains it
there preceded it   we knew we were free becuz   and maple syrup
less work when it rains   on account of paying it   ending in struggle
old-fashioned things there   newfangled hair to toenail   stole it from Wyatt
tongue depressor meant   Earp that is so famous there   signaled a height shift
caused by what must fall   how the moisture fills the air   principle of straws
then a little war   lycopodium powder   flashes like a bomb

it came pre-depressed   I turned it and that happened   it was all there was
then the mist closed in   voices were as close as ours   that is as our own
it's a death sentence   constructed in good English   closet of hangers
butted them like that   no — chiseled out a mortise —   tricked through a tenon
what does it matter   glue is a way to hold you   called twice in two days

Refusing to think

refusing to think   refusing for good reasons   no not for reasons
that's enough of that   quibble quibble over words   yes that's not the point
a green symphony   the American premiere   worth something some day
the bivoweled fluke   a red-snorkeled mammothnose   a humpbacked car seat
all for good reason   no not for that we've been there   illusion of dream

illusion of stew   the jailer woke ravenous   they're keeping costs down
you keep bickering   there was a near sighting then   slipped back behind bush
it was a birch dear   enough to befriend the wrens   enormous male thing
responded with rhymes   get a dictionary tic   yes you can TAKE it
yes you can MAKE it   in Leipzig, Lumumba Street   a genial marsh
murky pools and grass   someone has a nice wallow   let's see the bad one
oh that's nasty bad   it's like a circus with clones   that is, clouds, coigns, clods

then the back must go   I've ghosted along sweetly   will send the bats in
press here to recline   we found the wool shop district   next to the tinsmiths
next to blah blah blah   found a certain relief then   like for Hollywood
they all need music   *whee* is a technical term   they're forgetting us
well it's about time   you're acting like you could sleep   dreamily beguiled

SEVENTEEN

Our strings are Asian

our strings are Asian   that is the violin is   has that ancestry
to which history   the intelligence of sound   what human music
more than what birds make   a little bird on the ground   why would you then laugh
to sit in the hall   beautiful concert affair   and think of dry grass
mounded by that marsh   cool breeze weak sun early spring   waiting for the deer

who did never come   and thought of worlds without us   much too insincere
always fighting ooze   intuit indifference   hidden in the shrubs
springing out as night   could be Hollywood sound track   made unorthodox
a different zone   could have initiated   could think of one thing
overpowering   for those who feel shame deeply   to have it be swamped
with the beauty of   the here-nowness of pure gift   it is what love is
Valentine I'm Yours   who asked no questions no none   but offered and stayed

different from need   that aggressive agenda   out of liquid ground
the half-island life   take the lagoon as hunt-space   beating octopus
hundreds and hundreds   stew all day with tomatoes   oh Victoria
I have been my nerves   my ears accosted sleeping   had an early dawn
there was a pig thing   we got its heart hot and strong   Jenn-Air came later

Es lebe der Punk

es lebe der Punk   who's got that fancy white car   she's back from Milan
things keep slacking off   pretty soon we'll just *be* dogs   eating McDonald's
concepts kill wonder   who drives that little blue car   three men in dark suits
why did we feel smug   made a line for the phone booth   had to get the news
you want it to hold   to have something to crumble   because of anger

long live punk, punk lives   make your own repetition   how you know yourself
rarely surprising   oh but look here a glimmer   could be time to croon
say after me, I'M STRANGE   *a paleontologist*   a bisected arc
a little wrist flick   TV switches to music   stood at the altar
it came to knife time   we squelched those barbaric acts   the dog didn't know
stop kicking my dog   *every time I go to*   *town, boys keep kicking*
my dog around wah   Buffy St. Marie was that   lure of nostalgia

lure of apple pie   cure the problems of the world   Bosnia, taxes
lots of chains there too   you're going to lose Paris   magic will remain
you won't find it there   you won't believe it's still there   you'll think it's gone down
shaved his head and swore   they were all doing furies   they were all guilty
finally they left   we were interrogated   a sponge on my door

Is similar to

is similar to   Pandora's forbidden box   but no punishment
then not much like it   like saying orchards are like   Gardens of Eden
getting the wrong hold   going the wrong way from it   but who would have guessed
the ongoingness   sucked into typography   as a sweet instance
what began as gleam   ending with a stone triumph   *stone* as another

among clever ones   are the many matchmakers   bicycle riders
going downriver   finding a familiar route   but it rains so much
out the train's window   isolated villages   on the distant slopes
could be wine country   there's a gooey piece of gum   not just thumb-twiddling
hope that rhyme's sacred   hope that it isn't at all   like performed commands
she touches his cheek   he turns and touches her cheek   she turns back to where
this is a long play   finally they had all gone   it made *Seventeen*

a long list of rhymes   versus a long list of wrongs   too narrow to like
if it's not *figure*   it could be *having to wait*   it could be *TOUCH ME*
Professor Thomas   he's the one who said all that   I was so young then
I was quite old then   there was a backyard bonfire   yes they had hoses
burned eyebrows to nubs   drank Cokes afterward and shot   baskets at the church

Didn't have to give

didn't have to give   in blood advice up a hoot   gave it anyway
didn't have to watch   strangers kissing on TV   watched them anyway
didn't have to feel   happy clumsy stupid great   felt it anyway
didn't have to say   thanks excuse me you want to   said it anyway
didn't have to run   things away your business   did it anyway

you said I just shrugged   you were so angry with me   *giving up on life*
I didn't stand out   I did the things others do   you couldn't stand it
you thought I caved in   I didn't think it mattered   you saw a crisis
you wanted to say   DAMNATION ETERNAL DEATH   you didn't quite dare
that's when I got up   you didn't realize it   I was the winner
you made there be one   I was happy getting by   not building prisons
not building mansions   not the Great Wall of China   though that's a project

I'd enjoy causing   because you see it from space   someone has somewhere
with the naked eye   not that I'd want folks to die   but that's what happens
with these ambitions   suddenly the phone call comes   a man from Porlock
really Vienna   which probably explains IT   not that IT needed
he goes by humming   IT once sounded spectral-new   become classical

We came at it wrong

we came at it wrong   we squealed our brakes and dodged holes   we should have detoured
there were games waiting   no such event will recur   on autopilot
makes a slight delay   in the cycle of blinking   enough doors banging
traveled to Burma   picked out the worst wedding gown   that's my opinion
but got the right bride   canning as a food process   predating freezing

did you *pre-date* her   meaning *interview, size up*   meaning *come before*
which means something else   as if most of that didn't   retracts his canines
carnivores can smile   other animals cannot   that must mean whales can
who eat tons of krill   never seen one smile but they sing   birds are carnivores
but consider worms   okay that is sufficient   broke their greatest vase
the old Chinese one   guess I never noticed it   what with the strip shows
on all the channels   hard to steer clear and keep pure   hardly need the mags

all a riff on *wrong*   bunged it and left it done there   gotta move right on
going to be one   agents in the artists' house   for all you know then
swerving like dust storms   on this point erected walls   took promenades here
pumped like junipers   completely automatic   it reads it for you
it reads you for you   it has your privileges   it eats your supper

Wichita vortex

Wichita vortex   despite the storm went bowling   the sky turning green
we were all sexed up   you pouted a funny bit   being imperfect
waiting for the ball   fingering the vented air   to try for the spare
I kept my hands low   fingering all that I could   as you rose or sat
and when we got back   the night cleared out and cooled off   your street was blocked off

the tornado's path   near yours, your parents' back yard   a poplar row snapped
that was the date's end   everyone was unhurt   on that occasion
on others worse luck   as one night on a far road   off in the county
the cop car found us   you with your clothes all undone   such heavy petting
we weren't legal there   he made us move on but first   watched you get back dressed
his broad-beam flashlight   over your buxom body   his private peepshow
his gun, his office   acting like it was his right   I should have waxed him

that's what happened there   in the soft underbelly   of my America
heavy petting and   keeping away from the law   fighting the frontier
between desire and   gender the strange other love   breaking on the rocks
of that cold lighthouse   with its lonely importance   keeping itself free
but with things crumbling   a call to learn to talk still   without vocables

Auto accident

auto accident   killed one friend left one alive   who could learn nothing
no one there to blame   living friends tied together   tighter than by life
not having to talk   already on the inside   nothing to conceal
nothing to reveal   zeros all the outsiders   all such accidents
all violent deaths   from bombs from pricks of gunfire   knives and wires and clubs

as TV repeats   as films repeat books repeat   till we're all outside
inside and outside   to someone expendable   insignificant
faith is not growing   it's not even an issue   you can't buy it now
you can't fake it now   no you can if others wish   but you don't have it
you can fool yourself   but you know you really can't   not to say all do
not my grandfather   he said he wasn't afraid   he'd lived and kept faith
so that's possible   to die humbly, peacefully   if you don't lose faith

let's say you have faith   I don't see that that hurts you   I'm afraid of you
since you'll push on me   I know you shouldn't do that   and I know you will
even though you're wrong   wrong to push, wrong about faith   it's very charming
it becomes deadly   since you think I am so wrong   thus expendable
no more such essays   time to quit Mr. Nice Guy   have to learn to shove

Now I remember

now I remember   it was about rays falling   invisibly down
then there were pansies   tinsmiths repairing gutters   wielding an orange flame
we were at the door   we had to wait a long time   then pulled it open
there was another   we had to wait a long time   then pulled it open
there was another   we had to wait a long time   then pulled it open

behind us more guests   one had his own telephone   wanted to know rules
how to play poker   which bird will nest where and why   why wrinkles and who
an American   from the Flint Hills and long grass   from the wagon ruts
see a house so far   its Osage orange windbreak   its mulberry bush
from the pingpong room   from fire drills fallout shelters   land of fear and oil
with wind so planes come   land of grain elevators   of threshing combines
but no threshing floor   what it means to be Boaz   what being Ruth means

mid-English neighbors   the Clarks Merchants and Millers   and German Tholens
and Wiedemanns and   Achenbachs, then German Jews   and Armenians
and wherever the   Farhas were from and of course   Irish Moloneys
no Mexicans (no   Indians) no Indians   no one African
no Italians,   no Greeks, at least not nearby   not many swarthy

Threw a crew party

threw a crew party   whittled a sound boundary   despite his Honda
not so accustomed   would have to be envisioned   being a three-deep
can't see where it's from   (surrounded by organ sound)   his good bread slicer
excommunicate   went out back to wash her hands   made them walk and walk
knowledge relations   several access angles   came on a mission

had more storehouses   guess I missed that one come in   cats kept them busy
rejected the cool   rejected trilingual work   distanced from his claims
the Wimbledon plate   not worth such dedication   vaulted to an up
the moment before   pocketed all her faxes   took a simple cut
always deferred to   liking to climb up and down   so there was silence
here there was silence   a tradition based on "Love"   speaks in so vulgar
pushed into a car   didn't hurt him as would have   being pretending

being transcended   as we like to have meaning   transcending being
had done no weeding   nothing *made* them break apart   posed them eating one
he scraped off the crud   deciphered the Coptic script   parchment manuscripts
claimed to find a new   of course it's a very old   gospel of the truth
love as celibate   denigrate to masochism   self-loathing as God

An artist named Horn

an artist named Horn   the best place to pub-crawl here   most counter-tenors
special baritones   plans to go canoeing there   and mountain-climbing
release some daily   not still mad about the grapes   yes Handel used them
Bach just used altos   put on an exhibition   surrounded by pits
stacked up their trailers   Montaigne much too wonderful   to be so deadly

a diet of wine   making others do his work   estimated wrong
why they say *essay*   say *essay* say *essay* say   it sounds kinda French
disdained poltergeists   always fond of fresh-baked bread   even with no oil
pays Internet bills   connected to the thigh-bone   receding sarongs
he said *saranji*   he telegraphed but didn't   she's too compressing
nothing stays neat long   there's a women's toilet too   they had no taboos
or they *sold their flesh*   I was talking about theft   now it's business

I'm with Heidegger   threw her for a loop with that   his being thrown here
describing minutes   not summary, as we live   blanked out on sidings
on videotape   destroying a piano   *they can't call that art*
easy to figure   if the scales are harmonized   heard through the ceiling
a pleasure to give   you this award for being   such a fine person

Accepted their choice

accepted their choice   went the way they wanted to   couldn't be solo
explaining poker   having to write the rules down   screwed if you mess up
best thing is greener   wrote a home town tour guidebook   shot a video
excellent options   went deep for a pass too deep   got to FEELING GOOD
bought a souvenir   YOU MAY NEVER BE SO GLAD   paid with a Greek coin

an ancient Greek coin   that has got to be so dumb   raining on Derwent
Water raining on   Thirlmere raining on Grasmere   is famous for cheese
DING sorry but you've   lost and must now be shamed hard   please describe your stools
that's really too gross   look Mr. Executive   Producer next time
you bring a jackass   onto my show I'm going   to call him your name
I'll name your mother   I'll give your address your phone   I'll even say where
your daughters go to   school so you can fire me then   but you'll be exposed

change of frequency   it would have been so lucky   to have been here then
change of frequency   snowdrops in the town churchyard   by the war columns
the sons who were killed   and one whose father joined to   die two years later
change of frequency   which Abstract Expressionist   do you like the most
show how your pieces   relate to Dante/Vergil   do you write POEMS?

Kept explaining it

kept explaining it   kept laughing and retelling   telling newcomers
a certain district   of soft skin pleasant to touch   better than the rest
yes then I'll show you   something nicer than dining   he's waiting for us
in the theater   one who still writes notes and one   does it otherwise
otherworldliness   this-here-and-now-worldliness   head-to-head stuffing

studies in hyphens   chic studies in henhouses   crimps hearing of coops
boondock boundaries   grumpy breadwinners' revenge   just being themselves
he had to train her   she was pleasant but didn't   the bathroom's funky
deliberate slip   abortions are violent   true, legitimate
made it stand alone   affiliated music   descent to denim
thus to twill to warp   appearing diagonal   and serge, *serge de Nîmes*
smart people live here   I don't feel too much like it   I did my laundry

ate the specialty   tried to eat the specimen   hook, line, and sinker
never heard that one   can't find sweeter distractions   banged on her keyboard
banging hands on head   someone's aorta severed   wrenched in a quick death
easy now back back   memory of oranges   trees in Florida
balls of gold in green   nicer than Christmas almost   and the sugar cane

Considered giving

considered giving   considered being cabbage   being potatoes
thought of the insects   the gardener's attack modes   including plucking
squishing or drowning   considering a return   to earth-based prayer
earth-based medicine   a diet with brown-riceballs   that once in Boston
the then thereafter   never seen it in movies   rarely a war cause

they picked themselves up   necessary feminism   she criticized her
not without a sense   see at the end of the branch   there's where they shook hands
his faith in ponies   a man who owes men thousands   a woman of scarves
a set of five dwarves   kept busy on his birthday   got into a rut
bounced around in it   later found the main roadway   rain slanting on him
walked into London   Leslie Stephen as model   remembered sadly
Sino-Greek fabrics   creeping via Latin words   a whisper of grape

a romance of wine   down to intricate cellars   disposed of income
not wanting to have   the self-knowledge which they have   feeling too common
too over and done   terribly pleased to meet you   kept it at faceless
used the cosmetics   not quite getting the effect   which has one sole goal
not sex but money   using sex to make money   even when so old

The way they quarreled

the way they quarreled   never like in the movies   still more passionate
truncated and blind   not that the things they went through   perhaps others knew
and no one got hurt   not so bad as to need help   no E.R. at least
such as sex problems   money and pride and image   what do you desire
why can't you help me   hard to name those birds who've gone   got to have quick eyes

you need a swift tongue   you'll never have one so fast   you can simulate
she had a swift tongue   she swung it as a swordsman   why so impatient
I can't trust you now   weep weep weep weep weep weep weep   that's how it happened
she wouldn't have it   it was her choice but he'd have   alternatively
maybe he wouldn't   but previously she'd have   it didn't work out
fall anemones   views of other dry islands   almost worth a book
had operations   always a matter of trust   a girl will come back

who was it gave up   miracle that oracle   yielding's amorous
so is insisting   who had to learn how to dance   trailer performance
as recreation   everything is reviewed   parts children rehashed
staggering taxes   power difficult to chart   said Heraclitus
and said Confucius   and said Lao Tzu whoopdidoo   don't pull all the weeds

A long dark cavern

a long dark cavern   light torches along the way   how far will we go
save enough to leave   but there's no chamber of gold   so far as I know
the Greeks had a word   for an East Asian people   *Sēres* (the Chinese)
on which floor were built   Latin for silk (*sericum*)   and French *serge de Nîmes*
and thus our *denim*   but I can't explain the blue   of blue jeans or sky

in whose reflection   on a piece of glass I see,   quickly gone, a hawk
or just a buzzard   which cements together the   bow-sawn bass viol
its high harmonics   like the moose striding across   that shallow Maine lake
distressingly fast   which we had taken as deep   providing safety
and roofers at work   hammering syncopated   *that wonderful month*
fall of '82   just back from Sifnos we had   David and his gang
the Happy Roofers   climbing like they were monkeys   really rock climbers

smoking joints up there   the neighbors didn't complain   Maia was still one
I replaced a board   a fascia along the back   at first we served roasts
but later burgers   then just lentil stews and rice   they finished and left
home to Ithaca   that was all at the old house   where the next door boy
rode unicycles   and one night their shed burnt up   too close for comfort

Who found a steep hill

who found a steep hill   ascended by orange groves   as if by Matisse
in among jungles   criss-crossed by animal trails   creatures of habit
helpful to hunters   observe unawarenesses   ambush the stupid
this called strategy   the arts offer examples   playfields, practice grounds
we'll run counter-treys   *until they learn to stop us*   and so to defence

neither Goya nor   *Guernica* holds suffering   as we want it held
in an erasure   an embrace which removes it   completely like a
carpet stain cleaner   which really does restore that   new look of freshness
deep down things we lack   and keep almost finding YES   we almost get it
and those oranges   west and south of Vera Cruz   though far off seem close
close enough to twist   away gently off their stems   not to cart and sell
but to savor here   quartered with juice dribbling down   our hot dry bodies

I accepted him   using fair play as my rule   he was just a sneak
he could have been worse   it's hard to know with strangers   whence they get these films
he had his reasons   my assumptions too friendly   I don't feel lonely
they keep asking me   I don't think they really care   about something, yes
but not about me   let's say I'm fine, that I care   for you — *how are you?*

Threatening to freeze

threatening to freeze   things that were interesting   might be shriveling
there's a sheen around   pools and transmission towers   *will you still love me*
seemed to be a pop   she seemed to be undressing   a few men watched her
right in Venice Beach   Muscle Beach installation   many rube tourists
there it was a glaze   like a dessert only fades   this time a loud pop

we went to the show   first there were these huge fireworks   people drank and smoked
one guy got freaked out   he was mad at price gougers   talked him down to earth
if you won't love him   there's other's who will, she said   her vulgar ego
his romantic scorn   mini-loudspeaker we used   whose reach can broaden
and came the light show   gel filters fused to the beat   polychrome, shifting
it was what they wore   she loved her prom party dress   summed up America
devoted to it   joined up with excavators   learned to save his files

on top of the vein   must be exterminated   must risk the tunnel
ignore discomfort   wouldn't it be nice we said   to just look up there
somewhere in near space   and see your words created   as you typed by touch
that was before now   before brilliant glistening   the seasons skiing
you could break your hip   you're safe right now these last words   wrapping us around

About the Author

David McAleavey was born in Wichita, Kansas. At Berkeley in grad school he was poetry editor of *Occident,* and came to know writers such as David Melnick and Ron Silliman; at Cornell in the 1970s he helped edit *Epoch* magazine and played a major role in Ithaca House press. He has written scholarly works on the poetry of George Oppen, and he has taught (since 1974) at George Washington University in Washington, DC. His books of poetry are *Sterling 403* (Ithaca House, 1971), *The Forty Days* (Ithaca House, 1975), *Shrine, Shelter, Cave* (Ithaca House, 1980), and *Holding Obsidian* (Washington Writers, 1985); a recent chapbook is titled *David McAleavey: Greatest Hits 1971-2000* (Pudding House, 2001). He has edited two anthologies of Washington area writing.